—EVERYTHING ABOUT Timeshares

Before, During, And After The Sale

BY

WAYNE C. ROBINSON

DISCLAIMER

The information provided in this book, "*Everything About Timeshares: Before, During, And After The Sale,*" is intended to be a comprehensive guide and educational resource for readers interested in understanding the world of timeshares. However, as an author, I must emphasize the following disclaimer to ensure that readers approach the content with the appropriate context and understanding.

Not Legal, Financial, or Professional Advice:

The content presented in this book is for informational purposes only and should not be considered as legal, financial, or professional advice. While efforts have been made to provide accurate and up-to-date information, timeshare laws, regulations, and market conditions may vary across regions and change over time. Readers should consult with qualified legal, financial, or professional advisors before making any decisions related to timeshare purchases, sales, or other financial matters.

Independent Research Required:

This book is not a substitute for independent research. While it offers insights and guidance on timeshare topics, readers should conduct their own due diligence and research to validate and supplement the information presented herein. The timeshare industry is subject to dynamic changes, and readers are encouraged to verify information through reputable sources before taking any actions.

Personal Circumstances May Vary:

Timeshares involve a wide range of considerations, including financial commitments, contractual obligations, and lifestyle choices. The content in this book may not address specific individual circumstances. Readers should assess their unique situation, preferences, and financial capabilities before engaging in any timeshare transactions.

Endorsements and Testimonials:

Any endorsements, testimonials, or examples of experiences involving timeshares are provided solely for illustrative purposes. They do not guarantee similar outcomes for all readers, as individual experiences can vary significantly based on various factors.

Potential Risks Involved:

Timeshare ownership comes with inherent risks and responsibilities. While this book aims to provide a comprehensive overview, readers should be aware that investments in timeshares may carry financial, legal, and practical risks. As with any significant purchase, due diligence is essential to making informed decisions.

No Liability for External Links or Resources:

This book may contain references, links, or recommendations to external resources or websites. The inclusion of such links does not imply endorsement, and we are not responsible for the content, accuracy, or availability of these external resources.

Future Developments and Updates:

The timeshare industry is subject to ongoing changes and developments. While this book is accurate as of its publication date, subsequent developments may impact the information provided. We do not guarantee updates to reflect these changes.

By accessing and reading *"Everything About Timeshares: Before, During, And After The Sale,"* you acknowledge that you have read and understood this disclaimer. As an author, I urge readers to approach timeshare decisions with careful consideration, seeking advice from qualified professionals when needed. Remember that education and research are essential to making informed choices in the dynamic world of timeshares.

ACKNOWLEDGEMENTS

In the vibrant world of timeshares, where experiences unfold and dreams become a reality, I find myself overwhelmed with gratitude and joy as I pen down the acknowledgments for this book, *"Everything About Timeshares."* This journey has been nothing short of extraordinary, and it wouldn't have been possible without the support and inspiration of so many remarkable individuals and entities.

First and foremost, I extend my heartfelt thanks to the timeshare industry, which has been the catalyst for the remarkable adventures that have enriched my life. As a timeshare sales and marketing person, I have been privileged to witness the wonders of the world, surpassing even my wildest imaginations. The experiences and opportunities bestowed upon me by this industry have been nothing short of life-changing.

It is with deep gratitude that I acknowledge the personal development industry, which has been intertwined with my timeshare sales training. Through this connection, I have embarked on a profound journey of self-discovery and growth, unveiling a world brimming with endless possibilities. The transformative impact of this exposure has shaped the way I perceive life and has been invaluable to my personal and professional evolution.

To the thousands of timeshare owners who placed their trust in me, I extend my sincerest appreciation. Your faith in my abilities and dedication has been humbling, and I am forever grateful for the opportunity to make a positive impact on your lives. Your unwavering support has been the driving force behind my passion for this industry.

A special mention goes to the vibrant community of Facebook users who share a common interest in for the timeshare and vacation club industry. Your honesty and engagement have been a wellspring of inspiration, infusing fresh perspectives and ideas into this edition of my book. Your feedback has been a vital compass, guiding me towards delivering a comprehensive and meaningful resource.

To the eager students who enrolled in my timeshare cancellation video courses and books, I extend my heartfelt gratitude. Your honest reviews, feedbacks, and willingness to venture into a new frontier in the timeshare cancellation industry have been deeply encouraging. Your courage and trust have motivated me to pursue excellence in providing value to those seeking guidance in this domain.

Last but not least, I extend my appreciation to the readers of "Everything About Timeshares" book editions. Your openness in sharing your challenges and experiences as timeshare owners has touched me profoundly. Your stories have served as a powerful reminder of the purpose behind this book—to inform, empower, and make a positive difference in the lives of timeshare owners and consumers.

In conclusion, I stand indebted to each and every one of you who has played a role, big or small, in shaping this book. Your contributions have added depth, passion, and meaning to its pages, and I am honored to have walked this journey with you all. With heartfelt gratitude. Thank you all.

Wayne C. Robinson,
Author

FOREWORD

A lot has happened since *Everything About Timeshares* was first published in 2018. The industry consolidated as Marriott Vacation Club acquired Welk Resorts, Hilton Grand Vacations acquired Diamond Resorts, and Wyndham Destinations acquired the Travel + Leisure brand.

In 2019, a group of current and former timeshare members formed Timeshare and Resort Developer Accountability, Inc., a 501(c)(4) nonprofit focused on legislative efforts to improve timeshare sales and marketing practices. It was felt that there is no true consumer voice in Washington, D.C.

Charles Thomas, in Spain, recently launched *After Inside Timeshare,* a new independent website. Charles has published hundreds of articles, many submitted by timeshare members and owners, in addition to promoting the book, *Everything About Timeshares.*

Our combined worldwide efforts have promoted greater consumer awareness. Timeshares can be wonderful for families when sold properly and fully understood. However, a timeshare financed at 12 percent to 19 percent, with little to no resale value, can quickly spell financial disaster when the member is left with no option but to default. No one can guarantee an exit, and money-back guarantees are often not forthcoming.

Recording closings have increasingly been used against the buyer. The buyer is not allowed to record the sales session. There have been more than a few reports of sales agents and managers coaching buyers on how to "pass" Q&A. The buyer should record the sales session in states where it is legal to record without the other person being aware.

Many honest timeshare sales agents and managers have reached out, expressing their alarm as to the rise in unfair and deceptive sales and marketing as deeded timeshares converted to non-deeded, trust-based points, and private equity seized the industry. "Timeshare Sales" in 2020 appeared at number nine on the Federal Trade Commission's Top Ten Frauds list, and "Timeshare Resales" (fake buyers) came in at number ten.

Instead of victim-blaming, let's work together to build a better timeshare world. Wayne has improved that world by devoting countless hours listening to timeshare members, especially those who purchased in Mexico and the Caribbean. As we sail into a new timeshare decade, our resolution is to work towards better communication between members and developers and enhanced consumer education.

Irene Parker,
After Inside Timeshare

PREFACE

Welcome to the fourth edition of "*EVERYTHING ABOUT TIMESHARES: Before, During, and After the Sale.*" In these pages, I aim to shed light on the complex and often enigmatic world of timeshares while providing readers with the knowledge and empowerment they need to navigate this labyrinthine industry. My journey in the timeshare world began with enthusiasm and a desire to succeed, but as I delved deeper, I discovered unsettling practices that compelled me to take a stand.

My first steps into the timeshare industry were brimming with excitement. I joined a team at Angel Fire Resort in New Mexico, eager to sell timeshares and reap financial rewards. However, early on, I became disheartened by the dishonest tactics employed by some of my colleagues. The pressure to deceive potential buyers with false promises and lies was disconcerting, and it clashed with my integrity. I brought it up during an "integrity sales meeting" and ask why they were lying to clients to make a sale. None of the team of managers answered my question. Two weeks later, they fired me because, as they stated to me, "I was not a team player."

As my career unfolded, I worked for various resorts across different locations, witnessing both the wonders and the shadows of the timeshare realm. I prided myself on being an honest salesperson, but this often set me apart from others. Sadly, I witnessed companies operating without proper licenses, diverting funds, and engaging in unethical practices, all while preying on the dreams of unsuspecting consumers.

After generating millions for the timeshare industry, I reached a turning point. My conscience urged me to step away from a business that had lost its ethical compass. My decision to retire from timeshare sales was rooted not in regret but in a newfound conviction to help those trapped in the timeshare web.

This book is my effort to level the playing field for consumers. It is not driven by revenge, but rather by the desire to provide a comprehensive understanding of timeshares, dispel myths about timeshare cancellation, and arm readers with valuable insights that are typically hidden from public view.

Throughout these pages, I share insider knowledge gained from years of working within the timeshare industry. I've encountered both its allure and its dark side, and I believe it is crucial for consumers to be fully informed before making any timeshare-related decisions. This book unveils the truths often kept behind closed doors, empowering readers to confront any timeshare challenge with confidence.

Despite my commitment to transparency and consumer advocacy, I have faced attempts to silence my voice from participating in timeshare forums and social media sites. Certain corners of the industry prefer to keep these truths concealed, but my resolve to protect the interests of consumers remains unshaken.

I take pride in knowing that my work has helped countless families find resolution to their timeshare issues. The feedback and success stories from readers fuel my dedication to shedding light on an industry that has been tainted by deceit and questionable practices.

As you embark on this journey through the world of timeshares, I encourage you to approach the information presented with an open mind. Be prepared to discover aspects of the industry that may surprise you. My goal is not to dictate decisions, but rather to arm you with an effective weapon: knowledge. Armed with the insights presented in this book, you'll be equipped to make informed choices and navigate the timeshare landscape with clarity and confidence.

Timeshare developers, sales representatives, associations, and even cancellation companies have created a complicated web. Some are genuine, while others operate with questionable motives. My intention is to help you navigate through this complexity and emerge on the other side with a deeper understanding.

I extend my gratitude to all those who have supported this work and shared their experiences. I am honored to work for the consumer now, to provide a voice for those who seek truth and transparency in an industry that often thrives on ambiguity.

Let this book be your compass, your guide, and your shield as you venture into the world of timeshares. Together, we can unveil the truths, dispel the myths, and empower you to reclaim control of your timeshare journey.

Safe travels on this enlightening exploration.

Wayne C. Robinson,
The Author

TABLE OF CONTENTS

Table of Contents

CHAPTER 1

DEFINING TIMESHARES, TYPES OF OWNERSHIPS, AND LOCATIONS

Nobody wakes up one morning and decides to buy a timeshare, but a growing number of consumers spend an average of $21,000 to contribute to this multi-billion-dollar industry.

Timeshare purchases occur every day somewhere in the world: North America, Europe, Central and South America, Mexico, Caribbean Islands and Asia.

Many clueless consumers are lured into taking a timeshare sales presentation by mail marketing campaigns, on the phone, or while on vacation. They buy them in the city, on beach fronts, in ski resorts, in theme parks and now on cruise ships.

> *"ARDA says that the image of timeshare owners as elderly seniors playing shuffleboard has changed too, with timeshare owners becoming younger and more ethnically diverse..."*
>
> **Goldstein, 2016**

Consumers buy primarily for two reasons: Firstly, it is due to the alluring gifts offered by the developers. Timeshare resorts have been offering discounted accommodations (called minivacs) in exchange for travelers or vacationers to attend a timeshare presentation. This tactic converts into a high percentage of new owners.

Secondly, it is because of the sales and marketing staff. They are trained to gain the potential clients' trust, identify their dominant buying motives, and present an offer that makes financial sense. The industry's motto is *"sell on emotion, and close on logic,"* and it works.

In the United States alone, the timeshare industry continues to skyrocket despite the negative image it has earned over the years.

However, the demographics of the market have changed substantially in the last 20 years. Timeshares were generally purchased by the elderly or the nearly retired. Now, the demographics have changed drastically and are attracting younger families with higher incomes and more ethnic groups.

Amy Gregory, PhD, RRP and Tammie Kaufman, PhD published an article in *Developments Magazine* that presents a perception that Millennials have towards the timeshare industry. Although they reference original research that was published in the *Cornell Hotel & Restaurant Administration Quarterly* (February 2017), it presents an inaccurate reality of the timeshare industry by inexperienced students who are studying hospitality management at the University of Central Florida. Even the negative views mentioned in the article merely focus on the financial aspects of the industry.

> *"...There are distinct dimensions of the timeshare product that resonate with the Millennial generation. The attributes that the generation indicates as being most valuable align with their stated positive images of the product."*
>
> **(Amy Gregory, 2014)**

What the students and the authors need to be aware of are the realities of many "experienced" timeshares owners, and the legal battles that many timeshare companies are involved in because of unethical behaviors and illegal activities.

WHAT IS A TIMESHARE?

A timeshare is an ownership model in which many customers own allotments of usage in the same property. The timeshare model can apply to many different types of properties, such as condominiums, homes, campgrounds, vacation resorts, recreational vehicles, and private jets. (Investopedia, "What is a Timeshare?")

A *timeshare* (sometimes called a vacation club) is a property with a divided form of ownership or use rights. These properties are typically resort condominium units, in which multiple parties hold rights to use the property, and each owner of the same accommodation is allotted their period of time. (Wikipedia, 2018)

TYPES OF TIMESHARE OWNERSHIPS

Fixed Week or Deeded Week

A fixed week or deeded timeshare is a specific unit during a specific week within a specific season. Since there are fifty-two weeks in a year, most timeshare plans can only sell fifty weeks, as there should be two weeks available for maintenance for each unit. A family can own one or more weeks and occupy the unit during their allotted time.

With a deeded week, the owner usually does not need to make a reservation because the unit belongs to them and their family. The resort is considered their *home resort*. They can occupy that unit and bring others to enjoy it at no extra cost, according to the property's occupancy limits. If they do not wish to use the unit during their specific time, they can exchange the unit for a different time or different unit at the same resort or exchange into another resort anywhere in the world with an external exchange company (covered in a subsequent chapter).

Deeded timeshares are real properties and, therefore, recorded at the local county courthouse like any other real estate.

Floating Week Timeshare

A floating week timeshare is a unit that can be used anytime during a specific season, depending on the terms. It is also legally attached to a specific unit, usually to a deeded unit in the U.S., to prevent the resort from overselling the property. Oftentimes, the deeded unit is unknown by the owner unless it is specified in the documents. When the owner books a vacation in a floating week timeshare, they will not know which unit they will receive until they check in.

Like a deeded week owner, floating week owners can occupy a unit and invite others to enjoy it at no extra cost, according to the property's occupancy limits. If they do not wish to use the unit during the year, they can exchange their time into their home resort or into another resort anywhere in the world with an external exchange company.

Points System Timeshare

The points-based timeshare buyer is not an owner. They are members, such as a member of a country club or a gym. Those who buy points are right-to-use members, so they do not own anything.

A points-based timeshare is promoted as being the most flexible of the timeshare plans, as the owners do not have to travel one week at a time or at the same time. However, lack of availability is a common complaint. The points system is like a *timeshare currency* that can be used for as little as two- or three-day allotments rather than an entire week. With points, owners can occupy a unit and bring others to enjoy it at no extra cost, according to the resort's occupancy limits. Points are provided to the owner annually and can be used at one's home resort, accumulated, saved, or used to exchange into other resorts through an external exchange company.

Some points can be used for other travel-related products and services, cruises, shopping, and dining, depending on the terms. However, in general, the best value is obtained by using the points for their primary purpose—to occupy the resort. It is important for timeshare members to do their timeshare math, comparing the true value of alternative uses.

Travel Club Memberships

Travel club memberships are the surrogate twin within the timeshare industry. With a travel club membership, there are no guarantees. It is just that, a travel club, and members own nothing but air. The company usually does not own any of the resorts but merely leases the rooms from branded hotel chains.

Many timeshare owners are frustrated when they cannot book their vacations with their travel club memberships because there are simply not enough rooms available. Many believe that the entire property is a timeshare when it is not.

This is one of the reasons why travel club memberships should be purchased only at a minimum price or not at all. It is important for consumers to know exactly what they are getting into by thoroughly reading all the paperwork and researching the company.

If you purchase a right to use or a floating week timeshare that is not attached to a deed, chances are, it is not a timeshare but merely a travel club with very little inventory.

Timeshare is simply a general term that can be applied to any type, including travel clubs. Buyers need to beware of timeshare "trial" products because they may not be defined as a timeshare and, subsequently, may not be required to meet state contract rescission requirements.

When I was the director of sales and marketing for Prestige Travel Club at the Azul Sensatori Resort in Negril, Jamaica, I was informed by one of my trainers that guests are not purchasing anything but a right-to-use product. He called it "*air.*" The buyer owns nothing, and there are no guarantees.

I learned from the management of this 175-room hotel that the company only had a few rooms dedicated to the travel club. Most of the rooms were reserved for their all-inclusive guests, who were paying $500 to $700 per night.

Many timeshare owners do not realize that many of these properties only dedicate a portion of their inventory to timeshare. Therefore, there is limited availability in many resorts. This is why so many timeshare owners are frustrated when they cannot exchange when and where they desire.

Unfortunately for members, many rooms owned by timeshare developers can be booked online by anyone through any online travel sites and often with lots of availability for the same property.

The reasons are two-fold:

1. The property generates profits by charging nightly rates for their available rooms. If the property features suites, the prices can be as high as $700 per night, depending on the size, location, demand, and whether it offers an all-inclusive option.

   For example, I went online to the Manhattan Club's website to book a room. There were plenty.

   According to media reports, the Manhattan Club was fined $6.5 million by the New York Attorney General because of complaints by thousands of owners who were too often told that there was no availability for owners but plenty of availability for the public.

2. Because of this influx of hotel guests who can afford the high rates, they are prime targets for the marketing staff (disguised as concierges), who will lure these "whales" into a timeshare sales presentation.

Therefore, it is important to own a fixed week timeshare because the points system and the floating weeks have no guarantees. The owner has little control over their vacations.

TIMESHARE PROPERTY TYPES

There are a variety of property types within the timeshare industry, and each has its unique characteristics, amenities, and purposes.

The following are the most popular type of timeshare properties:

- ❖ Beachfront Resorts
- ❖ Cabins in the Woods
- ❖ Campgrounds
- ❖ Canal Boats
- ❖ Chateaus
- ❖ Condominiums
- ❖ Country Clubs
- ❖ Country Retreats
- ❖ Hotels/Resorts
- ❖ Houseboats
- ❖ Single-Family Homes
- ❖ Ski Resorts
- ❖ Ranches
- ❖ Recreational Vehicles
- ❖ And more …

TIMESHARE LOCATIONS

Timeshares are typically developed in busy tourist destinations and are located on every continent except Antarctica. The busier the location, the more timeshares are developed.

As more U.S. baby boomers retire and the influx of the millennial generation hits the travel and tourism market, there is a growing need for more timeshares that offer the opportunity to vacation whenever and wherever they please.

(Ktrinko, 2017)

Asia	Europe – Canary Islands & Cape Verde Islands	USA – Hawaiian Islands
Australia & New Zealand	Europe – Scandinavia	USA – Lake Tahoe and Las Vegas
Canada – Eastern	Mexico	USA – Middle Atlantic
Canada – Western	Middle East	USA – Midwest
Caribbean & Atlantic Islands	Northern Africa	USA – New England
Central America	South America	USA – Northwest and Alaska
Europe – Central & the Low Countries	South Pacific Islands	USA – Rocky Mountains
Europe – Eastern Mediterranean and Adriatic	Southern Africa	USA – Southeast
Europe – France, Italy & Malta	USA – California	USA – Southwest
Europe – Portugal, Spain & Andorra	USA – Central South	
Europe – UK & Ireland	USA – Florida	

CHAPTER 2

WHY THE TIMESHARE INDUSTRY AND VACATION CLUB INDUSTRY CONTINUE TO BOOM—REGARDLESS

Timeshares, or vacation clubs as they are commonly called, have been one of the fastest-growing segments of the travel and tourism industry. They have attracted mega hotel chains such as *Disney, Marriott, Hilton, Hyatt, Four Seasons, Sheraton,* and many others. Ritz Carlton also has timeshare, but it is referred to as *fractional ownership* or a *residence club*, a high-end product for a specific demographic.

According to some experts, seventy-eight million U.S. baby boomers are now retiring with a $1 trillion spending budget, and they are seriously considering the timeshare market to save on future vacations. An article written prior to the 2008 economic crash stated that U.S. baby boomers are the new target market for vacation clubs within the U.S.

> *"Once the economy turns around, hopefully in late 2009 or early 2010, companies will be salivating at the chance to pitch Boomers on the benefits of fractional ownership, as well as timeshare and vacation clubs."*
>
> **(Adam Kirby, 2009)**

In 2021, that forecast was surpassed, and the new target market is the millennial generation. Combined, vacation clubs are growing faster than they can fill the rooms.

According to a recent report, RCI, the world's largest vacation club exchange company, owned by Wyndham, continues to add more resorts to its worldwide portfolio. They now boast more than 6,300 resorts in one hundred countries with 3.8 million members worldwide.

WHY CONSUMERS CONTINUE TO ATTEND TIMESHARE PRESENTATIONS

Nobody wakes up one morning and decides to buy a timeshare. Many consumers know very little or nothing about timeshare, and some are aware of timeshare's negative reputation. Regardless, both groups continue to spend an average of $21,000 to contribute to this multibillion-dollar industry. This is done every day somewhere in the world: North America, Europe, Central and South America, Mexico, the Caribbean Islands, and Asia.

Clueless consumers are lured into taking a timeshare sales presentation through the mail, on the phone, or while on vacation.

Timeshare resorts have been offering discounted accommodations (called minivacs) for decades if travelers attend a timeshare presentation. This tactic converts a high percentage of new owners. Most consumers purchase a timeshare on the spot because of the sales and marketing staff. Sales agents are trained to gain the potential client's trust, identify their dominant buying motives, and present an offer that makes financial sense.

Incentives, updated programs, and slick sales and marketing professionals also attract those who already own a timeshare to buy another one. It is not uncommon for a timeshare member to own two or three timeshares. Additionally, some timeshare owners are trading

> *"...the U.S. timeshare industry increased for the 8th straight year by nearly 4% from $9.2 billion in 2016 to $9.6 billion in 2017."*
>
> **(Foundation, 2018)**

in their old timeshare for a different timeshare with new *bells and whistles*.

In the United States alone, the industry continues to skyrocket despite the negative image it has maintained for years.

THE GROWTH OF THE TIMESHARE INDUSTRY

The growth in the timeshare industry is built by the combined efforts of the travel and tourism industry, the creativity and vision of developers, and the variety of benefits and flexibilities offered.

Now that the entire industry is converting to a points-based system, there is more flexibility, allowing timeshare owners to vacation at more than one resort on one vacation and for shorter or extended stays. Points are like rewards points that can be used towards dining, merchandise, airfare, cruises, and other travel-related services. Typically, the best value for points is to use them as originally intended—to stay at the company's resorts.

The U.S. Growth

In the United States, the growth seems to stem from major brands buying up other brands. The major players in this capital-invested growth strategy are Hilton Grand Vacations, Bluegreen Resorts, Wyndham, and Holiday Inn Club Vacations. This becomes an attractive feature for new and current owners, as it provides more vacation locations.

The Mexico Growth

Mexico has historically been a favorite vacation spot for foreigners to escape the cold winter months and for spring breakers.

However, due to the cheap getaways offered by airlines and hotels, they are attracting North Americans throughout the year, even during "off-season" periods.

Despite the U.S. State Department's travel advisory against traveling to Mexico, Americans and Canadians continue to flock there. Consequently, more timeshares or travel clubs are being constructed in Mexico, particularly along the coastal regions of the Mayan Riviera and Los Cabos, to meet the growing demand of foreign travelers.

"The tourism business in Mexico is booming. The country's secretary of tourism announced recently that nearly 40 million tourists visited Mexico in 2017, and that number could continue growing at a rate of around four million a year."

(Times, 2018)

The Riviera Maya has become a vacationer's playground, and new resorts are filling up beachfront spots from Cancun beyond Playa Del Carmen. Luxurious all-inclusive resorts have been built along its white sandy beaches and at the edge of the Mayan jungle. They attract foreigners from all over the world, mostly Americans or Canadians, due to the short-distance flights.

Theme parks and natural parks are being built around the area. Many newer resorts have built their own theme parks on the resort property. For instance, Vidanta Resort (formerly Mayan Palace), located between Cancun and Playa Del Carmen, features a high-tech Cirque du Soleil dinner show called *Joya*.

The Caribbean Growth

The Caribbean has also seen an increase in timeshare resorts and partnerships formed between hotels and travel clubs. Again, with cheap flights, minivacs, and European travel companies such as Thomas Cook, developers are filling up the all-inclusive beachfront resorts. The Caribbean Islands are also booming, particularly in Jamaica and the Dominican Republic.

Brand name resorts such as SECRETS, ZOETRY, DREAMS, NOW, BREATHLESS, AZUL SENSATORI, ROYALTON, and GRAND PALLADIUM, are privately owned by separate companies. They partner with the travel club companies, inviting resort guests to a sales presentation through their concierge service. Everybody makes money.

Moreover, because the vacation club resorts are converting to mandatory all-inclusive programs that include food, drinks, and non-motorized activities, local restaurants are not getting the business they have in the past. Only a few souvenir and jewelry shops are generating an income, as most guests remain on the resort, oftentimes for safety reasons.

Nevertheless, the Jamaica travel club industry continues to boom as more resorts are being built, and foreign, primarily Mexican, travel club companies are partnering with branded resorts.

Cuba has been busy building timeshare resorts targeting foreigners, particularly Canadians, as the U.S. embargo continues to prevent American companies from doing business there. Mexican companies, such as Travelsmart, a division of Sunwing Travel Group based in Canada, have developed a travel club on the largest island in the Caribbean. However, like most travel clubs, they do not own any of the resorts. They merely rent or lease rooms.

The Asia Growth

Asia, also, has jumped on the timeshare bandwagon, as Asians have more disposable income. The Asian market has grown primarily because of the Chinese, who have more money and freedom than they had in the past.

> *"This type of vacation opportunity ... and the Chinese consumers are a perfect match for one another. The growing middle class has the disposable income and desire to travel."*
>
> **(Sellmytimesharenow, 2016)**

The India market has grown 50 percent over the past six years, appealing to a younger audience. RCI now boasts over three hundred resorts in India alone.

> *"After going through 'an initial phase of acceptance' during the 1980s, when it 'did not receive the required nurturing it demanded,' the product is now far more established, with younger people seeing the 'value of owning a timeshare and are eyeing it as a viable investment.'"*
>
> **(Adams, 2017)**

THE NEW TIMESHARE DEMOGRAPHICS

In the past, timeshares were generally purchased by the elderly, but the demographics have changed drastically. In the last twenty years, efforts have been underway to attract younger families with higher incomes and more ethnic groups.

> *"ARDA says that the image of timeshare owners as elderly seniors playing shuffleboard has changed too, with timeshare owners becoming younger and more ethnically diverse with a median age of 39 for owners, and more than 40% of U.S. owners either African-American or Hispanic..."*
>
> **(Goldstein, 2016)**

Despite the black eye that the timeshare industry has accumulated over the past thirty years, the industry continues to boom with more resorts being built, more amenities added, and more entertainment, food, and beverage options. Companies offer destinations that most people only dream of visiting. Within the timeshare industry, this is all possible and then some, and it happens every day somewhere in the world. When the decision is made based on accurate and reliable information, it is sound and can be of great benefit to a family.

Unfortunately, as you'll learn in a subsequent chapter, this is not always the case.

CHAPTER 3

THE 13 MOST SHOCKING SECRETS
OF THE TIMESHARE INDUSTRY

L ike any other industry, there are shocking secrets within the timeshare community that consumers are not supposed to know to protect the profits of the companies and the industry. There would be legal ramifications if consumers knew what really goes on.

Here are 13 shocking secrets of the timeshare industry that consumers should know about before they buy, sell, or dispose of their unwanted timeshares.

1. MANY TIMESHARE COMPANIES DO NOT OWN PROPERTIES

That's right. Many timeshare companies do not own the resorts where they sell their timeshares. They are owned by separate corporations and simply have an agreement with the timeshare companies to use some of their rooms.

When the members try to use their timeshares through the resort network or the exchange company, many find it very difficult because the timeshare has a limited inventory at that property. Consequently, there are a plethora of online complaints toward the company because there is no availability where and when owners want to vacation.

In the case of SECRETS, ZOETRY, DREAMS, BREATHLESS, NOW and SUNSCAPE Resorts in Mexico, the Dominican Republic and Jamaica, they are a collection by AmResorts. The company that sells the timeshare is Unlimited Vacation Club, a travel club, and they do not own any of the resorts. Consumers who purchase a UVC membership at these resorts are buying nothing more than an overpriced travel club membership that costs between $10,000 to $80,000.

According to the contracts, the legal entity for Unlimited Vacation Club is in Panama. Although it is a Florida based company, travel club members who want to mediate any legal action against the company must go to Panama.

Similarly, Prestige Travelers at Karisma Resorts and TravelSmart Travel Club in Mexico and in the Caribbean islands also do not own any of the resorts.

2. GUESTS WHO ATTEND A TIMESHARE PRESENTATION AND TELL THE SALES STAFF THAT THEY ARE NOT GOING TO BUY THAT DAY OFTEN END UP BUYING

When guests are invited to a timeshare sales presentation either by phone or while on vacation, they have no intention to purchase. When they share resistance with the sales representative up front, their chances of purchasing are even higher for two reasons.

Firstly, while guests attend the sales presentation, their guards are up, and they will show no intention to make a purchase. The objective of the salesperson is to lower their guards by being friendly and personable, and appear to be genuine. Once the guards are down, the sales rep is trained to identify the "real" objections that the guests have for not wanting to purchase that day.

Secondly, once the real objection is identified, the sales rep is highly trained to focus the presentation around that objection, find their "hot buttons or dominant buying motives," and come up with a sales strategy that will induce them to buy, that day. These sales strategies would normally involve coming up with a reason to justify lowering the price or giving them a free week of vacation or some other attractive gifts.

3. TIMESHARE ATTORNEYS AND RELIEF COMPANIES ARE GENERATING MILLIONS OF DOLLARS OFF TIMESHARE OWNERS WHO CAN EASILY DO THE WORK THEMSELVES FOR FREE

Timeshare attorneys and timeshare relief companies are generating millions of dollars in profits by helping timeshare owners get out of their unwanted timeshares. They use a variety of methods which begin with contacting the resort to initiate the process.

> *"... the Timeshare Exit Team. Its CEO, Brandon Reed, claims that it has a 99 percent success rate among the approximately 6,000 consumers who have sought relief over the past four years."*
>
> **Marks, 2016**

What most timeshare owners do not realize is that they can do the work themselves without paying anyone. In some cases, they can simply walk away without any repercussions because, in many cases, they do not own anything.

However, these savvy cancellation companies have popped up overnight and are generating millions of dollars in profits.

One timeshare attorney boasts that he has helped over 6,000 timeshare owners to dispose of their timeshare with a 99% success rate and charges an average of $3,900 per client. So, 6,000 X $3,900 = $23 million.

Although successful, the timeshare owners could have saved themselves the $3,900 and did it themselves by negotiating with the resort to transfer the property back with a warranty deed. This is the legal procedure that many timeshare attorneys use to transfer the timeshare back to the resort.

Timeshare attorneys and timeshare relief companies are so successful that the timeshare resorts have filed lawsuits against them because members are getting out of their timeshares through these companies.

> *"Several timeshare companies have declared war on attorneys and businesses that advertise timeshare cancellation services."*
>
> **Paul Brinkman, 2017**

One company, Mexico Timeshare Solutions, present themselves as a timeshare advocate and calls other cancellation companies scams. What their clients do not realize is that they are scamming clients into believing that they need their assistance to get rid of a Mexico timeshare when the clients can simply walk away without paying anything. Mexico timeshares are simply travel clubs, and companies cannot do anything to foreigners should they desire to simply walk away. This is how Mexico Timeshare Solutions guarantees their services.

4. MANY TRAVEL CLUB MEMBERS CANNOT USE THEIR OWN MEMBERSHIP BECAUSE THE RESORT HAS BEEN SOLD OUT – SOME MANY TIMES OVER

Many travel club members purchased because they wanted to travel around the world and explore new places and cultures. They will attempt to make reservations within their own resort system or use one of two of the largest timeshare exchange companies in the world, Resorts Condominiums International (RCI) or Interval International (I.I.).

> *"There are distinct dimensions of the timeshare product that resonate with the Millennial generation. The attributes that the generation indicates as being most valuable align with their stated positive images of the product."*
>
> **Amy Gregory, PHD, RRP and Tammie Kaufman, PHD., 2014**

One of the reasons why so many members want to dispose of their timeshare is because they cannot exchange where they want to go. The primary reason why many can't exchange is because the travel club's inventory has been oversold. With the points system, the resorts can sell as many points as they like.

According to a law suit filed against ILX Resorts. they oversold their inventory at the Los Abrigados Resort and Spa in Sedona, Arizona and that is why the owners could never get in. This is a timeshare, not a travel club.

> *"The elderly were induced to purchase vacation memberships in a same day sale without being advised as to the lack of a secondary market by intentional design. Memberships were accompanied by, at times, dramatically escalating maintenance fees."*
>
> **Insider, 2017**

Another lawsuit was recently filed against Diamond Resorts based in Las Vegas for securities fraud. The suit alleges that the resorts sell points that are not registered with the Securities and Exchange commission. Apparently, they are involved in a one billion-dollar lawsuit which accuses the company, and many of its affiliates of unfairly targeting the elderly.

Too often, resorts that sell a points system can easily oversell the inventory if the points are not directly attached to a deed.

Moreover, there are many resorts that simply have no inventory for their members because they prefer to use the rooms to market more guests to the timeshare presentations. This was the case with The Manhattan Club which resulted in a class action law suit by its members.

The points system and the right to use system are created for the advantage of the developers, not the consumers. They can sell as much as they like with little, if any, accountability.

5. MANY JAMAICA TRAVEL CLUBS ARE OPERATING ILLEGALLY AND DISCRIMINATE AGAINST LOCAL SALES STAFF

Although Jamaica has many travel clubs in the RCI and I.I. resort directories, Jamaica traditionally has not had timeshare legislation to control the industry. In fact, most travel clubs in Jamaica are operating illegally by not registering as a local business.

Daily sales are quickly disbursed to foreign bank accounts, circumventing the local banking system and the government. The Jamaican government might think that the resorts are selling the timeshares because they are registered with the local governments to operate as a legitimate business, but the travel clubs are not registered.

Jamaica has recently passed timeshare legislation to 'increase the presence of timeshare' according to a news article. However, the legislation does not include travel clubs that have already made their footprint in the country and might be operating illegally behind the skirts of high end resort brands, i.e., SECRETS, KARISMA and ROYALTON, which are separate entities.

They operate under the radar by working with small mom and pop businesses set up in the Free Zone of Montego Bay. However, the daily travel club sales are unreported to the local authorities. The Jamaican government may be losing millions annually in unreported tax revenue.

Moreover, they hire illegal foreigners to run the schemes and are mostly paid in banks in Mexico or in the Dominican Republic to avoid paying local taxes. Some may claim some income with the local mom and pop businesses, but what is presented does not represent the tens of thousands most foreign managers are generating monthly.

Most often, the travel clubs are not paying the local Jamaican sales staff with the same commission structure as the illegal foreign workers. While many foreign workers are generating tens of thousands per month, many of the local sales staff are barely making a living. This is undetected as the foreign workers are paid handsomely "under the table."

6. WHEN TIMESHARE OWNERS TRADE IN THEIR OLD TIMESHARES FOR ONE AT THE RESORT, THEY GIVE THEM ZERO TRADE IN

When an existing timeshare owner attends a timeshare presentation, they have the option of trading in their old timeshare for a new one.

The resort will offer a reduced price if the owner traded in their old paid-in-full timeshare. In some cases, they will offer tens of thousands for their old timeshare.

This is an old sales tactic used in the industry to make a sale. The closer will originally present a much higher price for the timeshare to make room for this "trade in."

In the end, the timeshare owner simply traded in one timeshare for another and paid the same price as those who didn't trade in a timeshare. TIMESHARE COMPANIES NEVER GIVE TIMESHARE OWNERS ANYTHING FOR THEIR OLD TIMESHARE.

7. MANY TIMESHARE SALES MANAGERS EXPECT OR REQUIRE THEIR SALES PEOPLE TO LIE, OR THEY GET FIRED

Many timeshare companies have a reputation for being dishonest, which is why there are so many lawsuits against them and so many disgruntled owners.

What consumers do not realize is that lying is expected in many resorts and required in other resorts. There are many lies within the industry that if the sales person does not present, he will not get the support of the management during the sales process.

The sales process is a team effort and requires the support of management to use a variety of sales strategies called such as "playhouse" to get the sale. Most often, if the sales person doesn't lie and his sales figures are not where the company wants them to be, the sales person will either be blackballed or fired.

All resorts have daily, monthly, and annual goals that they must hit – at any costs.

8. RACIAL, RELIGIOUS, GENDER AND SEXUAL PREFERENCE PROFILING IS A COMMON MARKETING TOOL

Timeshare resorts spend a lot of money on marketing costs to lure unwilling consumers to attend a timeshare presentation. The gifts must be attractive enough to convince even the most skeptical consumers to take a 90-minute sales presentation.

The gifts range anywhere from free vacations, free excursions to theme parks, i.e., Disney, show tickets in Las Vegas to cash. If the resort has a sales staff of 100, which is not uncommon in some places like Disney that has over 250, the marketing expenses add up.

Although the resorts get a nice discount from vendors, they must spend a lot of money to lure consumers into the sales presentations. Therefore, their marketing strategies must become a science – and a science it is.

Resorts will use many strategies to target demographic segments to get the most for their marketing budget. Within the U.S., they will target certain zip codes which could represent income bracket, educational level, race, and religion.

In Mexico and the Caribbean Islands, the timeshare resorts give their marketing representatives specific instructions as to what they are looking for. These instructions will determine the value of gifts they can offer to the guests, and the amount of cash the marketing representative will earn for bringing in certain profiles or guests who would most likely buy.

For many resorts, the most valuable couples are whites. The resort's marketing management will pay the most for a white couple over other races. Blacks, Latinos, Jews, Indians from India, men, and seniors will usually be offered fewer valued gifts and the marketing team will earn lesser pay when they bring in these couples.

Why? Because the primary purchasers in Mexico and the Caribbean Islands are the white from the U.S and Canada.

Surprisingly, in Mexico and the Caribbean Islands the locals are disqualified unless they appear to be wealthy.

9. MOST NEW TIMESHARE OWNERS SIGN LEGAL DOCUMENTS WITHOUT EVER READING WHAT THEY HAVE SIGNED FOR

After what was supposed to be a 90-minute sales presentation becomes a 4 to 6-hour arduous ordeal, consumers will give in and decide to make a purchase. Once they fill out the initial paperwork, they are emotionally drained and just want to leave.

However, it might take an additional 30 minutes or more for the final paperwork to arrive, especially when there are a lot of sales in the room. When the paperwork finally arrives, most new owners sign the paperwork without thoroughly reading it.

A resort chain in the Dominican Republic states in their 36-page agreement that if the owner shares any negative remarks or comments online about their experiences with the resort, the resort will cancel their membership. This is something that the new owners unknowingly agree to when signing the paperwork.

Many will also overlook the right of rescission period; the time allowed for the purchaser to legally cancel the sale and get a full refund. Sales persons are trained to prevent rescissions during this period.

10. WHEN NEW TIMESHARE OWNERS RECEIVE FREE ACCOMMODATIONS AND GIFTS AS AN INCENTIVE FOR PURCHASING THAT SAME DAY, THEY WERE ALREADY INCLUDED IN THE PURCHASE PRICE AND THE CLOSING COSTS

When the guests decide to purchase the timeshare, the resorts will list the closing costs in addition to the purchase price. It will not be listed as part of the purchase price, but added to the down payment.

For example, if the purchase price is $18,000, the down payment is 35% or $6,300. The closing costs will be an additional cost and could be as high as $2,000. Hence, your down payment could be $8,300.

The resort will use the closing costs to pay for the documents, the new owner's kit or packet, the exchange company enrollment, and any gifts that are offered as part of the deal. The remainder is often split amongst the sales staff involved in the sale.

For example, if the resort offers the new owners a free stay at the resort or other valuable gifts, they were already included in the purchase price or the closing costs. They are never free as they are presented.

11. CONSUMERS CAN PURCHASE A TIMESHARE FOR A FRACTION OF WHAT IT COSTS AT THE RESORT

Consumers who are serious about purchasing a timeshare should never purchase at a resort because they can buy the same timeshare for the same property at a fraction of the cost.

Resorts are charging exorbitant prices for a timeshare when consumers can quickly go online at the many timeshare resale sites and get it for much less.

While some resorts charge between $10,000–$20,000 for a timeshare, consumers can go online and purchase them for 10% of those prices.

Purchasing online also gives the consumer time to do the research and learn everything about the timeshare before making a purchase. There is nothing worse than making an expensive purchase at a high-pressure sales presentation and later regretting it. By purchasing online, one has the time to conduct their due diligence and pay considerably less.

When a consumer purchases a timeshare online, they will receive the same benefits unless otherwise documented in the paperwork. Read everything before you buy.

12. CONSUMERS WHO PURCHASE A TRAVEL CLUB MEMBERSHIP AT AN ALL-INCLUSIVE RESORT PAY MORE THAN THE GENERAL PUBLIC

Most Mexican and many Caribbean travel club properties are mandatory all-inclusive resorts that include meals, beverages, and some non-motorized activities.

This is an attractive feature for many consumers in some areas who would rather avoid searching for local establishments to eat and drink. With the all-inclusive option, they can eat and drink as much as they like without additional charges.

Many travel clubs operate within these resorts, although many don't own the resort.

When prospects attend a sales presentation, they are told that they will get a discount when they stay at any of the company's affiliate resorts. Some are even told that the timeshare will guarantee discounted airfares during their membership. This is a lie.

For example, if the guest bought a membership from the Unlimited Vacation Club that operates out of the Secrets Resorts, they can stay at any of the Secrets Resorts and get a discount on the mandatory all-inclusive options without paying a maintenance fee.

What the owners don't realize is that they are paying the same if not more for the all-inclusive than the general public is paying. When you add up the purchase price for the timeshare, and the nightly costs for the mandatory all-inclusive, they are paying much more than they can get on any travel site.

Many owners have gone online and discovered deals at the same resorts for a much cheaper price than what their timeshare offers.

13. ALL TIMESHARE OWNERS CAN EASILY GET OUT OF THEIR TIMESHARES, IF THEY KNOW THE PROCESS

Timeshare attorneys and timeshare relief companies are successful in getting frustrated timeshare owners out of their unwanted timeshares. Most will guarantee that they can get you out regardless of whether it is paid off or not.

Sadly, these companies use effective marketing strategies that include scare tactics to convince consumers to hand over their credit cards to pay for something they can easily do themselves as is the case with Mexican Timeshare Solutions.

KNOW BEFORE YOU GO ON A TIMESHARE PRESENTATION

Before attending a timeshare presentation anywhere, know before you go. Research the resort, the reviews, and the resale costs to learn all you can about the resort that has invited you.

If you want to complete your sales presentation in 90 minutes or less with your gifts, present them a copy of the resale and the negative reviews. They will usually get you out so that they can talk to a more willing prospect.

CHAPTER 4

THE LURING MARKETING TACTICS USED BY TIMESHARE AND VACATION CLUB DEVELOPERS

THE LOCAL MARKETING TACTICS

The moment you decide to attend a timeshare presentation, there is a 20 percent chance that you will buy—that day! If you are adamant and say to the sales or marketing rep, "*No matter what, I am not going to buy anything, no matter how good the deal is*," your chances of buying are even higher.

In the comfort of your home, you might receive a phone call or an invitation in the mail from a timeshare marketing company. They will introduce themselves in a friendly manner and offer you attractive gifts, enticing you to take a ninety-minute sales presentation in your area or a few hours away. They have your phone number, and they can call you for years, hoping to convince you to attend a presentation, unless you are signed up to a *do not call* list. Some callers will ignore the *do not call* list. They should be reported if they do. Of course, the objective is to make a sale.

Keep in mind that marketing reps speak to people all day and all night, and most people say no. It is a very high-pressure job that requires lots of training and quotas that must be met. As is true in any sales-orientated position, they lose their jobs if numbers are not met. Consequently, they do everything in their power to lure you into a sales presentation.

Some will offer a discounted rate at their resort or another resort in exchange for your attendance in a timeshare sales presentation. For families who live in big cities and do not usually vacation, this could be a great option to take the family on a weekend getaway and experience something they've never experienced before. Often, there is a multitude of amenities to enjoy, particularly for families with children who can spend all day in the pool while their parents attend a ninety-minute timeshare presentation that can end up as an all-day ordeal.

Foreign destinations such as Mexico and the Caribbean Islands might offer a minivacation (minivac) to get you to a presentation. This would normally include a discounted stay at their hotel and sometimes the airfare. Other incentives offered are digital music devices, TVs, radios, camping equipment, and many other items that appeal to a specific demographic, according to their marketing guidelines.

When you arrive, you must attend the sales presentation. The demographic of foreign vacationers results in a high closing percentage for the developers, so sales reps will do all they can for an opportunity to *pitch* to this group.

THE VACATION MARKETING TACTICS

When you're on vacation, an OPC (off property contact) is the person who may greet you and encourage you to attend a timeshare presentation. They have one of the most visible and fun positions within the vacation club industry. Their primary function is simply to bring in guests. They get paid just for bringing in "qualified" guests and paid again when a sale is made. OPCs work with the marketing managers. They work strange hours and sometimes in strange places. They must possess a strong sense of rapid rapport, creativity, and tenacity.

Assertive and sometimes aggressive strategies must be used to have a successful marketing campaign. Usually, attractive gifts such as cash, free activities, or discounts towards otherwise expensive excursions or entertainment are offered to potential guests in exchange for attending a sales presentation. In Orlando, one can expect free tickets to one of the theme parks. What do you think is the most popular theme park in Orlando? You guessed it—*Disney*. The OPC has a budget for each couple.

There are OPCs who stand by the front door of the resorts to approach guests as they attempt to leave for the day and bribe them with attractive gifts. Some gifts are small, but in some places, you can walk away with $300 or more in cash. A new resort in the Mayan Riviera of Mexico was recently offering $1,000 for taking a sales presentation. Beware! Some resorts in that region will not let you out of the salesroom unless you agree to buy something. Remember, you are in their country, and you're on your own.

Some OPCs demand a refundable cash deposit from the guests to ensure they will show up at the sales presentation at the agreed time and location. If they don't show up, the OPC gets to keep the deposit. OPCs can be found in airports, tourist booths, restaurants, shopping areas, busy tourist areas, cruise ship ports, and beaches. I have even discovered OPCs doubling as taxi drivers!

In some areas, particularly in the Caribbean and Mexico, they are stationed at airports under the guise of transportation, excursions, car rental agents, concierges, or some other visible position. They know all the flight schedules for each airline and know when to be at the right place at the right time. When travelers get off the planes and away from customs and immigration, guess who is there to assist them with transportation and excursions? You guessed it.

OPCs are posted at most vacation club resorts that are actively selling their product. They are typically females disguised as *concierges or hostesses* and will reveal their real intent once they connect with a guest. If guests refuse to take a sales presentation, they will continue to make attempts, even if it requires multiple phone calls to their rooms.

Once you agree to attend a presentation, the OPC will immediately become your best friend and help you with excursions and anything else to gain your trust. They are friendly, kind, and seem genuine. This is their job.

For them to get paid, you MUST show up. They will usually provide transportation for you to get to the resort. Once you have completed the presentation, they get paid. If you purchase, they get paid a commission with bonuses.

The qualified guests must meet certain "target market" requirements or criteria, i.e., age, sex, marital status, race, religion, income, and the quality of their accommodations. If you tell them you are staying at a hostel or a Motel 6-style property, you will usually not be invited. Historically, single men are usually not qualified guests, as they do not represent the typical profile of a timeshare buyer.

Each resort has its own qualifications determined by its sales track records. This industry spends lots of money to get you to a presentation. Therefore, they must keep track of who is and who is not buying. The quality or number of gifts offered will depend on the qualifications. For many resorts, certain races, nationalities, and religious sects are unwelcomed.

TARGETING U.S. MILITARY PERSONNEL AND THE DANGERS

According to Irene Parker, a timeshare volunteer advocate, military personnel is being targeted by timeshare and vacation club resorts within the U.S. with a sales pitch that they have a special deal for active military. They might go as far as stating that the resort developers want to show their appreciation for their service to our country by offering a special deal for military families. These "special deals" will come with a price.

I have obtained information that those military members who default on their timeshare obligations within the U.S. are being disciplined by their superiors and affecting their credit.

MARKETING TIMESHARE EXCHANGERS

Timeshare owners who exchange their timeshares for another resort will certainly be targeted to attend another sales presentation. After they check in, they will be contacted by the resort's marketing staff, who will set an appointment for them to attend a sales presentation. The marketing staff will lure them with attractive gifts in exchange for a one-hour sales presentation on what this resort offers compared to their own timeshare. The resort will often offer them an opportunity to either add to their portfolio or trade in their timeshare for a new one.

Timeshare exchanges represent one of the highest closing percentages for the industry, which is why many resorts will designate experienced timeshare sales reps to sell them.

THE HILTON AND DIAMOND RESORTS SALES AND MARKETING TACTICS

Recently, Hilton Grand Vacations acquired Diamond Resorts, becoming the largest upscale and luxury timeshare operator in a stock-based transaction. Hilton now boasts 710,000 owners, forty-eight sales centers, and twenty new markets.

Former Diamond members (380,000) can now use Hilton Grand Vacations properties and vice versa but with a catch.

From my experience in the timeshare and vacation club industry, there will always be marketing and sales strategies to generate more profit for the company, and this acquisition will be no different. One former Diamond member mentioned these tactics on a Facebook group page. She stated that they tried to encourage her to upgrade her membership to gain access to all of Hilton's properties.

Both former Diamond members and Hilton Grand Vacations members will be requested to attend owner updates. This is quite common for the industry, as 50 percent of the profits from the timeshare and vacation club industry are from owner upgrades. The sales strategy will probably be an opportunity for former Diamond members to use Hilton Grand Vacations properties if they upgrade their membership. Likewise, Hilton Grand Vacations members will also be requested to make the same updates to have full access to the former Diamond Resorts properties.

I advise readers to be careful and skeptical, as the resort's sales team will surely make attempts to upgrade their membership for a hefty price. They will probably use every trick in the book to generate more profits for the resorts by offering tempting "deals" to spend more money, including free stays, and upgraded rooms. Most often, if members have access to more properties, the maintenance fees might reflect this upgraded membership.

REFERRAL CONVERSIONS ARE VERY HIGH

Another tactic that most resorts use is referral programs, where they offer an incentive to owners if they refer their friends and family to attend a sales presentation. Many of the resorts where I worked had very successful referral programs that often resulted in very high closing percentages. Some referral programs offer friends and families similar gifts that they offer the public.

Royal Resorts in Cancun, Mexico, has a very satisfied customer base and members always refer friends and family. In fact, they accompany their friends and family to the sales presentation, encouraging them to buy. Of course, they prep them, tell them what to expect, and share with them the price they paid. Unlike most resorts, Royal Resorts owners all pay the same price. There was little room for negotiations. Royal Resorts was, by far, the most honest resort that I worked for. They guaranteed the same suite the same week for thirty years. Then, you get all your money back after thirty years.

The resort treated their owners so well that many would come back and buy more weeks. I recently met a couple that had three Royal Resorts weeks and owned another nine at other resorts.

The timeshare marketing process is a science that has been mastered by many timeshare developers. Millions of dollars of timeshare products are sold daily.

CHAPTER 5

THE STRATEGIES USED BY TIMESHARE AND VACATION CLUB SALES TEAMS TO GET YOU TO BUY "TODAY ONLY"

THE TIMESHARE SALES REPS' STRATEGY TRAINING

Within the United States, some state governments now require that the timeshare industry falls under the state's real estate division, requiring those seeking to sell timeshares to obtain a real estate license. This has done little to protect consumers but does demand a more rigorous requirement to sell timeshares. Requiring a timeshare sales agent to have a real estate license also generates state revenue.

If a license is required, the sales candidate must become familiar with the state's real estate and timeshare laws. This arduous process involves studying and passing the state exam. Some candidates attend professional timeshare or real estate schools.

Moreover, sales reps understand that if they lie during the sales presentations, they could lose their license, and both they and the resort can be fined. Unfortunately, some states, like Florida and Nevada, require proof of fraud. Unless the buyer recorded the presentation or has a "smoking gun" like written evidence, the member is dismissed with, *"Verbal representations are hard to prove"* or *"You have no proof."* People are sometimes literally pulled off the street to attend a presentation, and some are on vacation and may have their family in attendance, but the proof is hard to come by. Hence, the reason for this book is because public awareness is the only defense against a decision you may live to regret.

Some U.S. states do not require a license to sell timeshares, such as Virginia and Missouri. Neither the Caribbean Islands nor Mexico requires a license to sell timeshares. Travel club membership sellers don't either.

Why do people attend sales presentations? I have met timeshare owners who continually attend sales presentations, either because of the attractive gifts offered or because they want to trade in a timeshare or purchase an additional timeshare.

Many say they bought their original timeshare because of the patient, kind, and courteous sales staff, believing everything they were told. Well, that's the way they are supposed to be to make money. If they were impatient, rude, and discourteous, how many sales do you think they would make? The sales and marketing staff are hired based on their ability to present themselves as friendly and courteous to build immediate trust.

Timeshare sales managers hold daily and weekly training that requires sales reps to follow the sales presentation the way it was designed by the management, unless they have their own style of selling that produces a high sales volume. They are trained to do all they can to make the sale the same day. The last thing they want to hear is, "*I have to think about it.*" This is when the pressure builds up. The daily training includes handling objections and how to introduce a manager or closer to help close the deal.

Too often, these are not the most honest sales professionals. If the rep is selling, regardless of unsavory tactics, the sales management will reward them for their production. Some of the rewards include hefty cash bonuses, Rolex watches, and even automobiles. They may even be promoted to management positions.

Timeshares are generally a great vacation experience if they are sold honestly by well-trained sales agents who can guide the timeshare owners on the best way to use the timeshare. I believe greater honesty would give the industry the credibility it needs, though the industry seems to continue to grow despite the negative image generated by deceit and misrepresentations.

Timeshare resorts spend big bucks bringing in outside trainers to teach their sales and marketing staff to create the urgency needed to make the sale the same day. One of the most sought-after trainers is Shari Levitan, who has been training sales agents and managers for more than twenty years. Companies will pay upwards of $20,000 - $30,000 for her one-day training workshop. The resort can recoup that money within one to two hours after her training session.

Some larger companies, such as *Holiday Inn, Marriott,* and *Hilton* Vacation Clubs, have developed sales and marketing online courses to help train their staff.

Most resorts offer a daily SPIF (Special Performance Incentive Fund) the day after the sale for making the sale. In addition to their commissions and bonuses (covered in a subsequent chapter), this cash SPIF can range from as little as $40 per sale to as high as $300 per sale. A good timeshare agent could make as many as five to seven sales per week, depending on the tour flow and their sales skills. The training is crucial for improving product knowledge, handling guests' objections, and identifying the dominant buying motive of the guests to induce them to purchase that day.

RCI, INTERVAL INTERNATIONAL, AND ICE TRAINING

The exchange companies usually conduct a few hours of sales training to promote and teach their sales representatives about their products and services and ensure that all their sales reps are doing everything they can to promote and sell these products to new and current timeshare owners. They also educate the staff on how to clarify misunderstandings within the industry and introduce the new products, services, and resorts added to their portfolio. Usually, a local or regional RCI rep will conduct a mandatory presentation at the resort.

THE TIMESHARE SALES PITCHES

The timeshare sales process is different from most sales environments because the sales team only has a short time to make an enormous amount of money. Once the prospect is gone, the opportunity is gone forever. Therefore, it is vital for the sales team to master a variety of strategies for the diverse clientele. Each strategy is geared towards the close and is called a "pitch."

The Need to Vacation Pitch

In my fifteen years of working in the industry, I always thought encouraging families to take regular vacations was a good reason to sell timeshares. This is especially true for those who don't usually spend time or money on vacations. It gets them out of the house, away from their daily routines, away from work, and gives them an opportunity to explore the world.

According to numerous studies, most people only take half of the vacation time allotted by their employers, and for many, they take *staycations* or stay-at-home vacations. Health experts state that taking vacations helps with stress reduction, heart disease prevention, improved productivity, and better sleep. The EU, on the other hand, takes holiday time seriously. It has been said Americans live to work while Europeans work to live.

I especially enjoyed selling to families who were not taking vacations. Typically, the mother works hard to take care of the family, and most families these days are two-income households. So, when I had the opportunity to sell a timeshare to a family I felt needed to spend more time together, I tried harder to get the sale.

> *"It's time we say, "enough is enough" and learn to put our needs first. Taking time off is good for your mental and physical health, and you can come back more productive and effective. It's a win-win."*
>
> **(Daskal, 2016)**

Sadly, there are people, particularly men, who need to be forced to take family vacations. The timeshare sales presentation is designed to sell on emotion and close on logic. So, when it is time to show the money, it may be the husband who must be sold if the wife is already sold. Once the husband is showered with guilt for not spending enough time with the kids, extra goodies, and a deal that he simply can't pass up, the sale is made.

The Hotel Room vs. Luxury Suite Pitch

One major reason why consumers buy a timeshare is the better-quality accommodations and the amount of space they get compared to a hotel room. There's nothing worse than being on vacation in a hotel room with one bathroom, one television, and mom and dad sleeping next to their children with no privacy. However, with the rise of *Airbnb* and other booking services that can easily find you a condo or an entire home, that benefit is diminishing.

With timeshare sales, though, while the sales rep shows the resort and its facilities, guests are witnessing others enjoying it. You will often see children playing in the pools or engaging in arts and crafts, which provides a good selling point for families.

The sales reps flaunt the restaurants and other amenities the resort provides. Location is important. If they love the beach, show them the beach resorts they can visit as owners. If they love to ski, show them the ski resorts. A good sales rep will do all they can by listening to the wants and needs of the guests, *putting them in the picture* towards the sale.

Once a monetary figure is established that the guest estimates they will spend over the family's vacation lifetime, the sales rep will show an image of a two-bedroom suite and compare it to an average hotel room. Despite new booking alternatives, comparing a timeshare to a hotel room is still a valid point. The sales representative will use this to convince the guest that, for the same amount of money, the two-bedroom suite with a full kitchen, two bathrooms, three TVs, and a Jacuzzi is better than your average hotel room. The guests always agree.

After making numerous calculations over the years with several family lifestyles, I found that nobody could beat the overall cost of what they are getting for a timeshare compared to a hotel room. That seems to be changing under the points system, with many complaints of booking online being less expensive than using points.

For timeshares that are managed correctly, I believe considerable savings can occur by vacationing with a timeshare compared to a hotel. Families will usually go on the internet or contact their online travel agent and make reservations in a hotel room, according to their budget. They usually don't calculate the money they are spending that could be saved or better used by owning a timeshare. Most timeshares have a full kitchen, eliminating restaurant expenses. For families on a tight budget, food and beverage costs could add up to hundreds of dollars per vacation, which could make the difference of whether they vacation or not. Moreover, timeshares generally have more amenities than a traditional hotel, often available without cost.

My response to guests who objected to owning a timeshare due to the high cost is that when they own a timeshare, it doesn't require their vacations to be in some faraway location where they must take an airplane over an ocean. There are usually many timeshare resorts available within a half day's drive, where they can enjoy a nice vacation with their family for the price of a tank of gas and a quick trip to Walmart for their food and drinks.

In fact, the more you vacation, the less the cost, as you will learn in a subsequent chapter.

The Rent vs. Own Pitch

Buying a timeshare can be compared to owning versus renting or booking hotel stays. Financially, it often does make sense to own rather than rent. Buyers should consider the purchase price, annual maintenance fees, special assessments, interest on loans, and credit card debt to decide whether the timeshare presents a good value. In other words, is the price you pay for this scenario worth the usage? What are the long-term costs? In many cases, it is still a good value, especially when you know you're going to get a suite in a beautiful location where you can bring more people without the extra charges.

If you plan to take vacations over time, it does make sense to own, but you must weigh the costs between buying a timeshare versus using an online travel agency like Expedia.

The timeshare sales rep will always attempt to convince guests that owning is better than renting.

Again, weigh the costs. You cannot make that decision at the end of a ninety-minute sales presentation, much less one that has dragged on for hours. But people do it every day.

This is an illustration used to compare renting versus owning.

If the guests do go on vacations or are starting to vacation, the rep will ask them what they expect to pay for the average hotel rate.

Usually, this will range anywhere from $150 per night to $250 per night. Let's use an average nightly rate of $200. Great!

The next question is, how many years do you plan to vacation? They say they plan to vacation for the next thirty years. Great!

When you multiply the nightly rate of $200 times fourteen nights times thirty years, the total before inflation would be $84,000. Great!

Next, the rep asks the guests how much they think this price will change after inflation. Most will say about double. Great!

The figure to stay in an average hotel room for two weeks a year for the next thirty years with inflation is estimated at $168,000. The guest verbally agrees to this figure.

The rep now asks the guests, *"If it costs the same price, which makes more sense, renting a hotel room or owning a luxury suite?"* The guests usually agree that owning a luxury suite makes more sense.

While in the luxury suite, the rep will ask the guests three questions that will hammer the nail in the coffin to help close the sale:

1. *Do you like what I've shown you?*
2. *Would you use it?*
3. *If it was 100 percent affordable, would you like to become our newest owner today?*

Once the guests agree, the logic of the rent versus own scenario has been established. If they do not agree, the sales rep needs to identify the real objection—fear, trust, nonuse, etc.

This now leads towards closing the sale, which is focused on securing the down payment and establishing an affordable monthly payment.

The Timeshare Investment Pitch

Some sales reps will tell guests that they can write off their timeshare as an investment, and some people buy based on this false information. If a resort tells you that you can write it off, this is your red flag.

Yes, you can still save lots of money by owning a timeshare compared to booking hotel rooms, but for most, if not all, people, timeshare is not an investment and offers no tax deductions. The IRS will laugh at you.

Businesses can certainly write a timeshare off if they purchase it in the business name and use it for business purposes. They can purchase it for employees or management to take vacations or for clients, like any other business expenses. Many companies purchase vacation homes, condominiums, or yachts for their business that may qualify as a business expense. I always suggest consulting with a tax attorney or accountant. They will provide you with the truth. I cannot provide legal advice.

The investment advantage for owning a timeshare is investing in yourself and your family by taking vacations for better health and relationships. It is not a financial investment but more of an investment in your family time that can, when purchased properly, offer financial savings to get more out of your hard-earned dollars.

More family time is the only investment that a timeshare truly provides.

Timeshare sales team members are regularly trained by staff and outside companies to perform at their peak. It is a highly competitive environment, and those who are at the top generate more money than airline pilots, doctors, and lawyers. To reach the top, they must master the strategies typically used in the timeshare industry. In too many cases, this may include misrepresentation, fraud, and outright lying. In the U.S., the Federal Trade Commission defines this as *"unfair and deceptive trade practices."*

CHAPTER 6

HOW THE TIMESHARE AND VACATION CLUB EXCHANGE COMPANIES REALLY OPERATE

It appears that "exchanging" your timeshare for a different location is what most timeshare owners like about owning. This was probably the most attractive feature when I was selling timeshares. Most people wanted to travel to their dream locations at a reduced cost. This is the foundation of the popular rent vs own strategy sales pitch that all timeshare sales teams use.

I have since learned that many of you are not getting to your dream locations. One of the reasons is that where you own has low trading power - regardless of points.

Your (U.S.) contracts should state exactly which property your points are attached to regardless, where you purchased them. Ignore what you have been told, your location has everything to do with trading power.

Years ago, trading power was designated by colors. Now, with points, it is designated by how many points you own. It doesn't matter. A person who owns 10,000 points in Maui will always get better options than someone who owns 10,000 in the Poconos region of Pennsylvania.

Unless, the system has changed since I retired. I doubt it.

There are "dream locations" that many of you might not be familiar with or even considered. Most focus on one area in particular. Rather than focus more on where you cannot go, why not focus on where you can go.

Deposit your points/weeks, put in your dates, and see what's available. You might be surprised.

There is so much unused inventory around the world within the exchange companies (new resorts, adding on units, low season, not so popular destinations, etc.). Much of this inventory ends up as bonus weeks or "last call" weeks. They need to fill those rooms.

For example, rather than trying to get into Hawaii during high season, why not consider Hawaii during other seasons?

I spent a week just outside of Paris during January in a three-bedroom Marriott townhouse. It was one of the best vacations I ever had, and only a 45 minute train ride to Paris. I went into Paris with the local commuters.

So, rather than trying to exchange into Hawaii, why not consider other, not so popular places, i.e. Belize?

I spent a week in Caye Caulker, Belize, a beautiful Island in the middle of nowhere: Less tourists, the 2nd largest barrier reef in the world, and the location for the famous *Blue Hole* for divers. I swam with a group of 9 ft nurse sharks. It was great, and much cheaper than Hawaii.

Also, don't forget that there are many resorts that you can exchange to within a day's drive from your home.

I always told my clients that just because they want to take a vacation, it doesn't always require a lot of money and a trip across the world in a 747. There are many places that you can easily drive to with a tank of gas.

When I worked in the industry, I learned that the exchange companies will do all they can to get you where you want to go, if you are willing to give up more points. Back then, a two-bedroom could exchange for a studio in a high demand location. At least you got there.

Just curious. How many of you have visited your dream locations with your timeshares? Where was it, and where are headed next? Mark your answers in the comment section below.

EXCHANGING A TIMESHARE

One of the benefits of owning a timeshare is the ability to exchange one timeshare at another resort property in a different location with different amenities and even a different size unit in many cases.

For example, if your home resort is in the Ozark Mountains, you can exchange your timeshare for a resort on the Hawaii Islands. This is one of the benefits that timeshare sales reps boast about during the sales presentations. They will romance consumers with beautiful photos of luxury beach resorts, ski chalets, city hotels, cabins in the woods, and other environments where they can exchange their timeshare. This is the advantage of the exchange systems.

WHY MANY TIMESHARE OWNERS GET FRUSTRATED WITH THE EXCHANGE SYSTEMS

When consumers attend a timeshare presentation, they are often told that they can go anywhere at any time using one of the exchange companies, RCI (Resorts Condominiums International) or I.I. (Interval International). This is often untrue. Although many timeshare owners have successfully exchanged their timeshares through RCI or I.I., allowing them to travel all over the world to their chosen destination when they choose to travel, this has not always been the case for others.

By using exchange companies, members can leverage their initial expenditure to maximize their vacation dollars. However, like any other economy, supply and demand are paramount. This also applies to the timeshare industry towards exchanging where and when you want.

Neither the timeshare companies nor the exchange companies can guarantee anyone, regardless of where they own and in what season, where and when the member can travel. It all has to do with *supply and demand.*

Unfortunately, when guests make a timeshare purchase, most do not read the fine print in the exchange company's application, in part because this information is written on the reverse side of the enrollment form. Also, people are exhausted after the three- to six-hour sales presentation.

While you are at a timeshare presentation, you are told that you can go anywhere, anytime, particularly with the new points system, which offers more flexibility. They wow you with slick videos and glossy wall photos of families vacationing in some of the most desirable locations around the world. This picture is not always what results for some exchangers.

If you purchased a *Hilton Grand Vacations* points program, it doesn't guarantee that you can get into any *Hilton Grand Vacations* property whenever you want. It depends solely on the availability. This is not something they will reveal to you in the sales presentation. Like any timeshare exchange system, it also depends on *supply and demand.*

You might have purchased your timeshare in Hawaii, but your deed or ownership may be in Las Vegas, where the exchange power is less. You cannot expect someone who paid a lower cost for a *Hilton Grand Vacations* property in Las Vegas to have the same trading ability as someone who paid top dollar for a *Hilton Grand Vacations* property in Hawaii. The timeshare companies will never admit this standard practice.

The *supply and demand* scenario is true for both external and internal exchange companies. If you purchased a timeshare in the Pennsylvania Poconos and want to exchange into Paris, the chances are slim to none, simply because there is not enough demand, from a global perspective, for the Pennsylvania Poconos.

Likewise, if you purchased your timeshare in Orlando, which has a high demand, and you want to go to Paris, the chances are also slim because of the oversupply and the competition against the other timeshare owners in Orlando. Again, the key to the timeshare economy is s*upply and demand.*

INTERNAL EXCHANGE SYSTEMS

Most timeshare resorts offer an exchange network for owners to exchange within their resorts network for a different time, unit, or size. This allows the timeshare member greater flexibility.

If the timeshare is deeded, they "own" a specific time, unit, and size, and they must contact the resort to exchange unless there is a network amongst the owners to exchange amongst themselves.

Some resorts charge a small fee, depending on the terms. This is in contrast to the points buyers. In most cases, points buyers are "members" like a member of a country club or gym.

The advantage of the internal exchange is that owners can travel to other places within the resort's network. For example, if an owner is deeded in California and the resort has a property in Hawaii, the owner can exchange their week for Hawaii.

Many timeshare developers also allow their members to exchange their timeshares for hotel stays if the company owns hotels, i.e., *Marriott Vacation Club, Hilton Grand Vacations,* and *Hyatt Vacation Club*. For a small fee, they can exchange their deeded, floating, or points ownership for a hotel stay for as little as two nights rather than the entire week.

EXTERNAL EXCHANGE SYSTEMS

More often, timeshare owners will join one of the external exchange companies to trade their timeshare for another timeshare somewhere in the world outside of their resort's network. The two largest timeshare exchange companies in the industry are Resorts Condominium International (RCI) and Interval International (I.I.).

The exchange companies do not own properties. They act as travel agents for the timeshare industry. Members can elect to give up their points or week of timeshare for a timeshare at another location around the world within the exchange network. They can also arrange for other travel-related services such as airfares, cruises, hotel stays, and car rentals.

Each exchange company has its own website where members can view their account information, review the properties within the network, request an exchange, or pick up extra weeks.

The RCI Exchange Company

RCI is by far the oldest and largest exchange company in the world and is the exchange company for more than 6,300 properties in 110 countries around the world.

The company has a slick and easy-to-use website where members can view what is available for exchange or trade. The site features resort photos, full descriptions, and reviews from other RCI members. It also includes tourist activities and places of interest for each destination. Members can view their past and future exchanges, the number of weeks they have deposited, and other information about their accounts.

For a timeshare member to exchange into another property, they must deposit their timeshare week or points with RCI to exchange it for another property within RCI's network. Usually, but not always, if the member owns a studio unit, they will get another studio, and so on, for a one- or two-bedroom unit. If they are applying points, each resort requires different points depending on the unit size, location, season, and demand.

There are no taxes, service charges, or tourism charges, as you would find with booking many hotels, but RCI charges an annual fee and a fee to deposit the week.

The RCI website is www.rci.com. RCI is owned by Wyndham Hotel Corporation.

The Interval International Exchange Company

Interval International (I.I.) is the second-largest timeshare exchange company in the world and boasts over three thousand properties in seventy-five countries around the world. They are owned by Interval Leisure. Sometimes, RCI and I.I. represent the same developers. *Disney Vacation Club* Resorts used to be with I.I. but switched to the RCI network.

While working as a timeshare professional, I discovered that Interval International resorts seemed to be of higher quality, not always, but often. For example, they include the *Marriott Vacation Club* properties that are not with RCI.

Interval International has a program that allows members to see what is available for an exchange before giving up or "depositing" the member's own timeshare.

The I.I. website is www.intervalworld.com

- ➢ San Francisco Exchange Company (SFX Preferred Resorts)
- ➢ Dial an Exchange (DAE)
- ➢ Resorts worldwide. Free to join. No annual membership dues.
- ➢ Platinum Interchange
- ➢ Over 1,300 resorts worldwide. No annual dues. Low-cost fees.
- ➢ Resort Travel and Exchange
- ➢ Resorts worldwide. Membership based.
- ➢ Worldwide Timeshare Exchange

> ➤ U.K based. Traditional weeks exchange system. Discounted bonus weeks and rental service.

> ➤ Trading Places Xchange (RTX)

> ➤ Resorts worldwide. Membership based.

Cruise Exchanges with the Exchange Companies

You can exchange your weeks or points for cruises, but you typically pay more using your points than the public pays. Do not waste your time—unless you want to throw money away.

CHAPTER 7

THE TRAP—
THE COMPLETE TIMESHARE AND
VACATION CLUB SALES PRESENTATION

While you wait for your salesperson to take you on the sales presentation, you will fill out some preliminary information about yourself, show your credit card, and give it to the friendly receptionist. They may also ask for your I.D.

Remember, you may have been told, *"It's not a sales presentation,"* and *"It's only ninety minutes."* Know that it is most definitely a sales presentation, and few escape a timeshare presentation in ninety minutes or less unless a purchase is made within that time.

One appalling tactic is to take your driver's license and credit card and refuse to return them. Some companies require their staff to make copies of the credit card and the driver's license or passport. When you demand they return the card and I.D., they dodge the subject, or another member of the sales tag team is brought in to start over. Tenures of six to eight hours are not that unusual.

They may have had you sign a small form agreeing to the ninety-minute presentation and indicating the time. Read the fine print. It may state that by signing the form, you agree to be robocalled. Once that starts, you can expect a lifetime of aggressive and annoying calls.

When you arrive at the scheduled time, you are probably a little nervous and unsure of what to expect. All sales agents go through the same process to gain your trust—the greeting, the warm-up, the intent statement, the survey questionnaire, the program, and the property tour. The end goal is to close the sale. Not every resort operates the same way, but this is typically how the process went at the resorts where I worked.

Master timeshare sales trainers like Shari Levitan charge tens of thousands of dollars for sales training sessions. This is what she has been presenting for over twenty years:

THE MEET AND GREET

Your salesperson meets you. They smile and shake your hand. This is your first impression of them, so it must be as good as the sales agent can make it. Their job is to warm up to you quickly and have you warm up to them.

The Warm-Up

The sales agent will whisk you away to another location (typically a salesroom, restaurant, or a quiet area). They will initially show genuine interest in you and your family. This is the warm-up. They might get you to talk about your vacation, why you have chosen that destination, your hotel accommodations, the city you live in, or any other light conversation to get you to like and trust them.

THE INTENT STATEMENT

Then, they will tell what to expect during the presentation. They will also tell you that they expect a *yes* or a *no* at the end of the presentation. TODAY is the operative word. You cannot think about it, only a *yes* or *no*. They are trained to handle either response.

The intent statement will typically be like this or something similar:

> *"John and Mary, we want to thank you for visiting our beautiful resort. We are going to spend a little time getting*

to know each other. I am going to show you how our program works, show you the beautiful suites, should you become an owner with us today, and then show you the prices. All we ask is that you give us a simple yes or no today. Is that something we can agree on?"

THE (DISCOVERY) QUESTIONNAIRE OR SURVEY

If there is a meal, they will use this time to warm up more or begin asking questions about your vacation lifestyle. If there is no meal, they will go right to the questionnaire. This is their way of identifying your *dominant buying motives* and *hot buttons*, which will be used towards the close.

Here are some of the questions they typically ask to determine your hot buttons and which sales strategy to use. The questionnaire usually takes about fifteen minutes:

- ❖ What is your occupation?
- ❖ Do you have children?
- ❖ Do you take vacations? Why or why not? If not, why? If you do, why?
- ❖ How much do you spend on your accommodations?
- ❖ How many more years do you see yourself taking vacations?
- ❖ Who do you travel with?
- ❖ To what destinations have you traveled?
- ❖ Where would you like to go on future vacations?
- ❖ Why haven't you taken vacations?

❖ What type of rooms do you normally stay in?

❖ Do you own a timeshare? If yes, where, how much did you pay, what are your maintenance fees, and why did you buy it?

These are the "bullets" they will use against you at the end of their presentation to sell you that day. Keep in mind that the presentation is an *emotional sale*. If the salesperson discovers that you do not vacation, then they will try to use guilt or some other emotional tactic to get you to buy. If they learn that you do vacation, they will convince you that their way is cheaper and better and that you deserve it. You are sold on the idea *emotionally*, while the close will be made on *logic*.

THE TIMESHARE PROGRAM

By now, you are seated in a large room amongst many other sales presentations. The room has a nice buzz with lots of excitement, upbeat music, champagne bottles popping, and announcements of new sales.

They might place you in a theater to watch a video, or they will show you how their program works at the table, the benefits of ownership, and the exciting destinations that you can visit using exchange companies. They will explain how easy it is to exchange and how much better their program is compared to your current vacation plan. Location is usually their selling point if it is a beachfront, mountain, or city.

THE PROPERTY TOUR

After they've explained their program, they will take you on a tour of their beautiful resort. This initiates the *emotional* part of the sale, like getting into a new car for a test drive. They make you feel as if you already own it. They will show you all the amenities that owners enjoy: the pool, activities, bars and restaurants, games and social events, the fitness center, and anything else. They will especially point out anything they have identified as your *hot button*, such as the kids club where your kids can enjoy activities with other children or the discounts you get at the bar or restaurants, should you become an owner.

At the end, you will be gracefully escorted into one of their luxurious suites, where they might even ask you to sit on the sofa or their branded bed.

Next, come the "trial closes" designed to elicit "yes." It works! They will most likely ask you the following three questions:

1. *Do you like it?*

2. *Would you use it?*

3. *If it is 100 percent affordable, would you like to own it today?*

THE CLOSE

After you agree that their program is better than your current vacation lifestyle, you will be shown a price that is normally ridiculously high. They will label it as their *regular price,* and they will wait for your response. It will always be *"No way."*

If the salesperson does not show the TODAY prices, they will get a manager (closer) to close the deal. This is where the pressure begins.

Let's suppose that the "anytime" price is $75,000. Using the figure concluded in Chapter 4 of this book ($168,000), you will agree that $75,000 is a better deal.

However, if you buy today, they will possibly drop the price to $45,000, a savings of $30,000. In this scenario, they could go down to $28,000 for the same product, but you are not supposed to know this. At this point, they will try to extract the real objection, which could be easily done by asking, "Why not?" Your responses might be:

1. *You want more time.*
2. *You never do anything without sleeping on it.*
3. *You never make financial decisions without speaking to a professional consultant.*
4. *You will think about it.*
5. *You need to discuss it with your kids and many other excuses.*

If the closer is not getting you to bite, which is expected, they will come in with another "drop." The price could drop down to $20,000.

They might justify this drop with a few reasons such as:

1. *We had a couple who purchased last year who defaulted because they could no longer afford the payments. You just pay the balance they owed.*

2. *We had a couple who just upgraded to a bigger unit, so we can sell their old unit at their original price.*

3. *We can trade in your timeshare to give you equity. This will bring down the price.*

At this point, if the closer can't make the sale, they may bring in another closer who will have a better deal for the same two-bedroom unit that was originally $75,000, but now only $18,500, if you buy today.

There are a variety of creative and strategic ways they will use to induce people to buy on the spot. They've already determined whether the couple can afford it or not. They have discovered their *hot buttons* earlier that can be used to get them to buy that day. This information was cleverly collected during the "survey." They could justify lowering the price again by offering an *every-other-year* program. They could also throw in more gifts or issue a collection of RCI weeks for only $199 each (worthless). This is one reason why the ninety-minute presentation takes hours.

THE MAGIC OF DELETIONS

You're in the salesroom, and the sales rep either explains how their program will benefit you and your family or shows you the goodies you will receive if you buy today.

There are other couples in the room, and there is a lot of noise. You're not sure if this is a scam and will not give in. You will stick to your original decision not to buy anything, no matter how good the deal is.

Suddenly, a champagne bottle is popped, and the cork flies across the room. The announcer says something like this: "*Ladies and gentlemen, may I have your attention, please. Help us welcome our newest members, John and Mary, from Los Angeles, California!*" The crowd applauds and looks around for the newest owners. They may not exist.

This charade is called a "deletion" and is a tactic used to inject excitement into the room. It is designed to push those who are a little skeptical over the edge. They want you to think, "*If everybody else is buying, then it must be okay.*" In marketing circles, this is called the "bandwagon" effect.

HOW TO GET OUT OF A TIMESHARE PRESENTATION IN NINETY MINUTES OR LESS WITH YOUR GIFTS

There are many ways to get you out of the three- to six-hour "ninety-minute" timeshare presentation. After all, ninety minutes was what you agreed to when you accepted the offer. Both parties should honor the agreed-upon ninety minutes.

Bring Children

There is nothing better than a restless child to get you out quicker. One Facebook poster shrewdly advised not to bring any clean diapers if the guest has a baby. Timeshare salespeople will do everything they can to prevent the child from interrupting their sales process, including taking the child away, giving the child to another salesperson, or placing the child in a room with other children. Don't do it. Keep the child with you because the sales staff will want you and your children out of the salesroom, especially if your child is upsetting other salespeople and their guests.

Show Resale Copies

Show them copies of resales for their resort. You can print up a copy from your computer. Call or visit the website of a member of the *Licensed Timeshare Resale Broker Association* before you attend. The members of this organization charge no money upfront to list a timeshare. Plus, LTRBA members understand all timeshares, so they can offer comparisons. http://www.licensedtimeshareresalebrokers.org/

Pull up the resort on the website and show the sales agent the lowest price on the site (i.e., $2,000). Ask them if they could beat that price. They cannot. If they tell you that resales are no good, then tell them you would never buy something that has no secondary market. You're out of there.

Time Is Up Close

There is nothing more annoying to the salesperson and management than a guest who is standing up and ready to walk out of the door. You have given them your promised ninety minutes. They need to give you your gifts. If your ninety minutes are up, you can simply go. It may not be that simple, though, when professional sales "tag-team" agents try to get you to start over. The new sales agent or manager attempts to reset the clock. This is not fair, but it happens. *"Wait, I'll need to get my manager before you go,"* is a common ploy.

Tell them that you would never trust or do business with a company that has already broken their first promise—a ninety-minute presentation.

They will ask you to sit down so that they can bring in another closer with a "better" deal. If they ask you to wait for another person, CONTINUE STANDING. You have fulfilled your part of the agreement, and there is no sense staying any longer unless you have questions or want to purchase their product.

DO NOT SIT DOWN. If you do, they are in control. If you remain standing, you will draw a lot of unwanted attention from the sales staff and other guests. REMAIN STANDING or BEGIN WALKING towards the management and ask them where to pick up your gifts. If they ask you to sit down for a few more questions or to arrange for your gifts, DO NOT SIT DOWN. Continue standing. They will quietly escort you out of there.

Too often, timeshare salespeople are coerced by their management to keep guests at the table until another closer or a "better deal" is on the table. That is why many resorts keep people for hours. The problem here is that either the couple is too embarrassed to leave, or they are just being kind to the salesperson. Often a warm relationship has developed between the guest and the sales agent. They don't want to insult the agent who has been so nice to them.

Well, let me be the bearer of the bad news.

They are only nice to you for one reason ... $$$

CHAPTER 8

HOW TO BUY A TIMESHARE...
ON YOUR TERMS

BUY ON YOUR TERMS, NOT THEIRS

Only buy on your terms, not theirs. Timeshare salespeople will always tell you that their offer is good only for that day. This is not true. You can return the next day or later and get the same deal—always.

Your terms should be as follows:

1. Always record the entire sales presentation. At the end of the day, you are responsible for what you sign. Local law enforcement, consumer protection agencies, state departments of real estate, and each resort developer only recognize what is written in the contract, not what was said during the sales presentation.

2. You want to have full access to the resort's website during the entire rescission period. Unfortunately, too many new owners or members do not have access to the website, and when they learn that it is not what they thought or were told, it is too late. The rescission period has ended.

3. During the closing process, ask to be removed and review the timeshares for sales at that resort on www.sellmytimesharenow.com. Most likely, the listed prices will be a fraction of what the resort is asking. Show them the listing and ask them if they can beat that price. By this time, the sales presentation is over.

4. You only purchase if you are guaranteed in writing that you can confirm a reservation at their property whenever you please, so long as you provide enough notice. This

only applies to buying a fixed or floating week. It rules out a points-based program, as they cannot guarantee a reservation. Availability is based on supply and demand.

5. After researching the resort reviews and the resale market, you will know the market value and negotiate from there. Be sure to ask about the benefits or lack of benefits of buying directly from the resort as opposed to secondary market points or weeks. Stay away from timeshares that have virtually no secondary market. Imagine buying $100,000 worth of timeshare points today, and ten years later, something happens, and you need to sell, but the secondary market does not exist. Similarly, what would happen to the primary housing market if the secondary market didn't exist?

6. Determine whether you want an every-year or every-other-year usage.

7. Timeshare developers will add closing costs on top of the purchase price. Do not pay the closing costs. Ask them to deduct it from the purchase price. Closing costs are bonus money for the sales staff. Vacation points are a right-to-use product, like a country club. There should be no closing costs at all. If you purchase a vacation club in Mexico or any of the Caribbean Islands, there should be no closing costs or maintenance fees, as they typically do not own any of the properties where they sell.

8. Ask for a copy of the maintenance fees over the past ten years. They can always provide it unless they have something to hide.

9. If you decide to purchase the timeshare, read the entire contract. If there is not enough time, don't buy it. Some things cannot be determined by reading the contract, like over-promised availability.

10. If you did make the purchase that is eligible for rescission and regret it, then two days before the rescission period ends, proceed to cancel the purchase. They should always reduce the price to their bottom line just to get the sale. This is where you want to be. Negotiate from a position of strength. If a new contract is prepared, make sure they restart the rescission period as this is a new contract. Beware that some trial products do not have a rescission period in some U.S. states, like Nevada and Missouri.

11. Ask if you can sell or transfer the timeshare to another party. What are the procedures and the costs? Try to find out in your research if you resell the timeshare, will the new owners get all the benefits. If they don't, then why buy? EVERYTHING should be in writing or don't buy at all.

THE RCI OR INTERVAL INTERNATIONAL CREDIT CARD TRAP

If you are on a timeshare presentation but do not have the full down payment when you want to purchase, they may arrange for a loan with monthly payments until the full down payment is received, or they'll encourage you to apply for a credit card through RCI or I.I.

In the U.S., Barclays Bank is often the credit card vendor. If a credit card application is approved, the new credit card can be used for a full down payment or, in some cases, the entire purchase.

Avoid paying for the entire purchase using a credit card because if you are in a dispute later, your dispute is with the credit card company rather than the timeshare company. It's easier to cancel a loan with a timeshare company than to cancel credit card debt because the credit card company did not sell you the timeshare.

To further encourage consumers to apply for a credit card, the credit card companies will offer you a low introductory interest rate for the first six to twelve months. Some offer 0 percent for a period of time, but the rate will go to as high as 24 percent after the interest-free period. A luxury item should never be financed at 12 to 24 percent.

Think twice about the financial responsibilities you are about to incur.

THE EQUITY (TRADE-IN) EXCHANGE SCAM

An effective strategy during the timeshare sales closing process involves the equity exchange or trading in your existing timeshare for a new timeshare. This is a great sales tool to overcome the objection from guests who would like to purchase but have already bought a timeshare before and do not want to possess two. If the guests prefer the new timeshare but want to get rid of the old one, an *equity exchange* is an option. The resort will offer to give equity for the old timeshare to purchase the new one. It's not uncommon for guests to own a timeshare that they wanted to get rid of anyway.

Sadly, too many naive guests buy into this "equity" scam.

It doesn't matter what you own, what price you paid, or where you bought it.

NO TIMESHARE COMPANY IS GOING TO GIVE YOU ANY MONEY FOR YOUR TIMESHARE—PERIOD. But you can use your current timeshare as leverage to get them to reduce the price considerably.

Here's how it works:

Like any sales transaction, there is a bottom-line price. Timeshares are no different. There is a bottom line for every studio, one, two, or three-bedroom or beyond. The objective of the timeshare sales process is to get as much money as they can without going below the bottom-line price. This is why owners pay different prices for the same product. If the sale goes below the bottom line, the difference or loss will come out of the salesperson's commission, or the deal will simply not go down at all.

Let's suppose that the ANYTIME price is $45,000. But the TODAY price is only $25,000, supposedly saving you $20,000. Although this might seem like a good incentive, the guests might still resist and not buy. So, they will try a different strategy—a trade-in.

The information gathered from the survey at the beginning of the presentation about the guest's timeshare ownership would be secretly shared by the salesperson to the closing manager, who would then fill out a *"trade-in"* sheet to present to the guests later. The manager will use this tactic to "justify" a trade-in amount.

The sales rep may inform the guests that they will give them "equity" or buy their timeshare if it is paid off. They may offer the guests $5,000 for their timeshare. Now, the price is only $20,000. If the bottom-line price for the timeshare is $15,000, the company still has $5,000 before they reach their bottom line. The deal goes down as $20,000, and the guests will go for the deal, thinking that they have a great deal, but still overpaid $5,000 above their bottom line. The guest could have purchased the same timeshare on the resale market for a fraction of that price.

Even if the guests continue to resist, the company still has $5,000 to offer as further incentives: a FREE week at the resort, a "free" vacation elsewhere. Regardless of the deal, the GUESTS ALWAYS PAY FOR THE EXTRA GIFTS, either in the purchase price or built into the closing costs.

The guests will sign away their old timeshare for the new one, believing the company took in their old timeshare. Sometimes the company doesn't fulfill this promise, so they are now stuck with two timeshares and two maintenance fees, and there is nothing in the documentation that details the deal. It only specifies the new purchase price of $20,000. Some contracts will state that the company is not responsible should the traded-in timeshare not transfer to the company.

Nevertheless, if you are genuinely interested in purchasing the new timeshare, use the current timeshare as leverage. Inform them that you have decided to keep your current timeshare. The deal will still go down with the same $20,000 price because, in actuality, the company did not give you anything for your old timeshare.

This is the perfect scenario to demonstrate the pressure that has become common in today's timeshare industry.

SIGNING THE PAPERWORK

The purchase agreement will include all the information needed to prepare the documents. This document would include the purchase price, sales tax (this can also be used in negotiations), closing costs, and the payment schedule if you agreed to a loan. The closing costs can range anywhere from $499 to over $2,000. This money is used for the exchange enrollment, new owner's kit, and gifts, with the remainder usually split amongst the sales staff, depending on the resort and the deal. The gifts are NEVER free.

Once you have signed the purchase agreement, they will take your credit card and identification to start the paperwork. During this time, they will usually have you fill out some preliminary paperwork, agreeing to the terms. Be warned that some companies will make a copy of your identification and credit card, which is illegal in many countries.

When the contract arrives, you are usually sent to a VLO (verification loan officer), or they will come to the table after the champagne has been popped and you have been announced as the resort's newest owner. They will explain the paperwork. Alas, it is now hours after the presentation, and you want to just get the heck out of there. Few people read the contract. They just sign and leave.

I worked as a VLO at one resort whose agreement was thirty-six pages. Who would want to read that while on vacation? Nobody would or does. Most people initialed each page and signed the documents without even reading them, at best a cursory glance. This process could take as little as two minutes. They were unaware of a rescission period, and they unwittingly agreed not to make any negative comments about the resort online, or their contract will be canceled, and they will lose their investment.

You must know where the contract is legally enforceable. Foreign developers, especially travel clubs, are known for setting up corporations in Panama or other offshore regions. If you have a legal issue with them, this is the only place you can legally resolve it.

THE RESCISSION AND CANCELLATION PERIOD

The *rescission period* is the time allotted by local governments for consumers to review their purchase and legally cancel their timeshare. If they cancel their purchase during this period, the government requires timeshare companies to give purchasers a full refund of any monies they have received.

However, there is nothing more frustrating for a sales team than to spend 6-8 hours to make a sale that later cancels.

Anywhere in the world, except Aruba, when you purchase a timeshare, there is a rescission period or period of cancellation. This is the time when you should be able to get out of your contract with a full refund.

According to a *Redweek* article, Dr. Amy Gregory, assistant professor at the University of Florida who has been studying the impact of buyer regret, remorse, and rescission decisions, many timeshare buyers regret their decisions.

The article mentions that 15 percent of timeshare buyers rescind, which is the norm for the industry, according to Jeff Weir and Dr. Gregory. Although Dr. Gregory's research includes "interfering information" that

> *"A whopping 85 percent of all buyers regret their purchase (for money, fear, confusion, intimidation, distrust and other reasons)."*
>
> **(Weir & Redweek, 2017)**

causes purchasers to cancel during this period, the article doesn't mention the internal tricks resorts use to deter people from canceling.

When guests desire to cancel, the manager or closer involved in the sale will attempt to talk them out of it. This attempt could involve lowering the purchase price, offering more gifts, reminding them of the dominant reasons why they purchased or lying to prevent them from canceling during the rescission period. For many, this conversation can be intimidating and embarrassing, especially for purchasers who befriended the salesperson.

Once the rescission period is over, the purchaser has often lost their original deposit and will be liable for full payment. The salesperson is usually not concerned about the customer once the sale is complete.

I have worked for some resorts where the managers would adamantly state in the morning sales meeting that they were not returning any funds, period.

Most of the time, the salesperson or the VLO (verification loan officer) will explain the contract in a way that will prevent canceling. They may attempt to embarrass you. They may even advise you, at that moment, not to sign the contract if you are thinking about canceling. This persuasive tactic is called a "*take away,*" as it lowers the guest's guard. People usually move forward and sign.

You have the right to cancel the contract within a certain period—usually five to seven business days, depending on the state, province, or country. Whether you are in the U.S., Canada, the Caribbean Islands, or Mexico, you can obtain a full refund if you exercise your right of rescission *in time*.

What is often overlooked in the paperwork is the clause stating that you must pay for all the extra gifts they have given you should you cancel. The resort may charge you the retail price for any extra gifts, free rooms, excursions, or anything else they used to bribe you. So, if they offered you a free stay at their resort and you cancel, you might have to fork out rack rates on that hotel stay, and this could accumulate into hundreds or thousands of dollars.

Remember, you signed the contract, and they have your credit card information. What's more, you have given them permission to do this in case you cancel. *Read all the paperwork.*

I suggest you always read the entire contract before signing anything or take advantage of the rescission period provided by the local government. This is a way out. Don't allow the resort or the salesperson to make you feel guilty for canceling. You're the one who is going to be stuck with this for possibly a lifetime, not them.

They've already made their commission the moment you signed the contract, and they make good money.

Remember to cancel your auto-pay on your bank or credit card if you decide to cancel within the rescission period. Some cancel their checking account and open a new one, as stopping the payments is not always easy.

WHAT TIMESHARE COMPANIES DO TO PREVENT CANCELLING DURING THE RESCISSION PERIOD

In addition to losing their commission from a sale, many timeshare sales teams feel that they could have spent the same time coercing somebody else who might purchase and not cancel. Therefore, they will do everything they can to prevent new owners from cancelling their timeshare purchase during the rescission period.

Here are 5 strategies that many timeshare resorts use to prevent new timeshare owners from cancelling during the rescission period.

1. *They will avoid the rescission clause that is included in the documents.*

Although the rescission clause is clearly written in the documents, many timeshare agents or Legal Verification Officers (VLO) will avoid mentioning this very important item.

The resort's management will not allow sales reps to mention the rescission period during the sales presentation. This could lead to disciplinary action or getting fired.

While reviewing the paperwork with the new owner, many reps will discuss other matters to avoid the clause that outlines the rescission.

After 6-8 hours of grueling sales presentation, the last thing the new owner wants to do is to review all the legal jargons included in the documents. Most of the time they are not aware of the rescission period if it is never mentioned by the staff, and thus preventing sales cancellation.

2.   They will follow-up to overcome Buyer's Remorse

It is important for timeshare sales staff to keep in touch with their new clients shortly after the sale to prevent them from cancelling during the rescission period. Most clients will have buyer's remorse and reconsider their purchase. After all, it might have been a very expensive unexpected purchase that was sold on emotion.

Buyer's remorse often happens after they have taken the time to think over their purchase, research the company that they had just spent $21,000 with to ensure that they did the right thing. For this reason, sales reps need to be available just in case the client wants to cancel.

Some sales reps will treat their new owners out for a nice dinner to help "bond the relationship." This tactic works well as the new owners are getting to know the sales agent on a personal basis rather than a salesperson. After all, the salesperson took his or her own money and time to take the new owners out for a nice dinner. Why would they consider canceling with "their new friend?"

3. They will follow-up with a "friendly" phone call

What is typical when new timeshare owners are on vacation is that some resorts will require the sales staff who made the sale to meet with the new clients the next day, or to call them within 24 hours. This is to overcome buyer's remorse, or in case the new owners have any further questions or clarifications. Usually, the new owners forget the verbiage during the presentation and the salesperson needs to explain the program again.

4. The resort will reduce the sales price.

If the new timeshare owners decide that they want to cancel, the resort will offer to reduce the price.

A preliminary cause of buyer's remorse is that the new owners didn't take the time to review all the documents and to absorb everything that was said during the sales presentation. After all, they didn't think that they were going to buy.

Often time, this "second round "rendezvous could last another 2-3 hours of negotiating, but many take the bait and purchase at the lower price or keep the original agreement.

Unfortunately, the timeshare company may not change the original rescission period, and the new owners now have less time to reconsider their purchase.

Consumers need to be aware that the "today only price" offered will always be available the next day, week, month or years later. Don't be afraid to return later. Resorts will not turn down the potential for a sale if it doesn't exceed their bottom line.

5. *The resort may offer more gifts...for a price*

If the new owners want to cancel, the management can offer more gifts to "sweeten the deal." These free gifts might include free accommodation, free meals, free activities, free or discounted RCI weeks or other options.

New owners must be aware of the new terms that might have entered into the contract. These terms could include paying rack rates for the free accommodation or paying the highest advertised prices for any gifts just in case they decide to cancel the deal. This action could add to thousands of dollars if they decide to cancel.

Therefore, it is imperative to read all the documents thoroughly before signing or presenting it to an attorney during the rescission period.

Conclusion

The rescission is the consumer's right to cancel and terminate the timeshare purchase. Although timeshare resorts will use every strategy that they can, including embarrassment and condescendence, it's the consumer's final decision to end the relationship or move forward with it.

It's tantamount to a girl breaking up with her boyfriend who has spent all his time and energy wooing her. She discovers more about him and decides to terminate the relationship. He will use every tactic and strategy that he can, including embarrassment and condescendence, but in the end, it is still her decision to terminate the relationship or move forward.

Depending on the government, the rescission period can be anywhere from 3 days to two weeks.

THE EXIT PERSON (DEVELOPER'S REPRESENTATIVE)

If you decide not to purchase that day, then you leave and get your gifts? No. There is one more hoop you must get through before you get your gifts, the developer representative (exit person). This is the person responsible for getting you your gifts, or so you were told. This is simply another sales pitch to earn your business.

They will greet you warmly and ask you some questions about your experience, particularly why you didn't buy that day. Once you have answered the questions, they will offer you a less expensive program.

This "trial program" can range anywhere from $500 to well over $3,000. It is usually a week at their resort with access to the exchange company. But, when you use it, you must return to one of their resorts for another sales presentation. You can take it and opt to get your original gifts for attending this "ordeal," and you are done. Remember, some states, like Nevada and Missouri, offer no rescission period because the trial product is not defined as a timeshare. Buyers should still attempt to cancel, especially if they were sold by deceit.

Do your due diligence, take your time, and get exactly what YOU want on YOUR terms. Know what you are buying.

CHAPTER 9

THE BEST AND WORST PLACES TO BUY A TIMESHARE OR VACATION CLUB

LOCATION, LOCATION, LOCATION! NONSENSE!

Yes, location is important up to a point but does not necessarily determine where you can exchange. Decide where you absolutely want to vacation, and that will be the best location to own a timeshare.

Regardless of where you own, you will compete with other members when you attempt to exchange into other areas. This can be frustrating when the salesperson sold you a red week on the beach and told you that you could go anywhere at any time. Technically, this is true but only if where you want to go is *available*.

The value of your timeshare and the exchange possibilities have everything to do with *supply and demand* for the resort where you want to vacation and the *supply and demand* of the resort where you own your timeshare, regardless of its location. No one can guarantee where and when you can use your timeshare unless it is a fixed week, and you vacation at that property during that week. This is the major benefit to fixed week owners, especially in vacation hot spots like Hawaii.

You can own the most beautiful and expensive penthouse suite in the area, but if you bought a timeshare in upstate New York in winter, your exchange chances are going to be limited. Why? Because the exchange company must believe that somebody wants to vacation at your timeshare during the time that you own. Even if you bought a floating week or points, it is always attached to a unit and week. Look at your paperwork. This doesn't mean that you can't go on vacation somewhere else, but availability might be limited.

One good thing is that many empty timeshare slots around the world need to be filled. There are always possibilities but less if you buy a winter week in upstate New York or any off-season, unpopular time.

My advice is to purchase a fixed week timeshare at a resort and location that you wouldn't mind visiting repeatedly. You can purchase your timeshare near a beach, at a ski resort, in a city, or even on a houseboat or canal. A fixed week is a guaranteed week that no one can take from you because you own it. Unlike the points system, which is a right-to-use product, fixed-week buyers buy actual real estate. This is why we call fixed week buyers "owners" and points buyers "members" because they don't "own" anything.

If you don't want to use your timeshare in any particular year, you can deposit the week with an exchange company. The resort can then rent that week out to generate income and bring in new guests to market their timeshare program.

Even in Cancun, some resorts still sell fixed weeks. Royal Resorts is one of those companies. They have six resorts to choose from in Cancun, Playa Del Carmen, and the Dutch Caribbean islands of St. Maarten and Curacao.

THE TIMESHARE RESALE MARKET

There are thousands of timeshares for sale all over the world. Timeshare owners want to sell their timeshare for a variety of reasons. Many timeshares are offered online for as little as $.077. That's right. You can buy a timeshare today that costs a timeshare buyer thousands of dollars for under a dollar. Timeshares bought on the secondary market may have a reduction or elimination of benefits. Buyers should thoroughly research restrictions before buying a timeshare from the secondary or "resale" market.

The good thing about the resale market is that you get to choose exactly what timeshare you desire without being pressured during a multi-hour timeshare presentation and paying top dollars. You can get the same timeshare with the same benefits for a fraction of the resort's asking price. A member of the Licensed Timeshare Resale Broker Association can explain the differences in buying from the developer direct compared to buying a resale. (Sell My Timeshare Now harms many by charging $1,400 or more to list timeshares known to have little to no secondary market.) Timeshares are listed by resort name, country, unit size, and resort photos.

Redweek.com and *TUG2.com* also have timeshare resales or timeshare rentals on their sites. So do other online sites.

There are many timeshare resales for sale for as little as $1, as the owners just want to be rid of them. This is a great buy because as a member of the exchange companies, you have access to the bonus and getaway weeks, as do other members, regardless of where they own. It is truly an open market for exchange members.

Before making a purchase, this is what you need to know:

- ❖ Is the price negotiable?
- ❖ If it is deeded, when, where, and what size?
- ❖ If it is a points system, walk away.
- ❖ Review the resort reviews and complaints.
- ❖ Who pays the closing costs?

❖ What are the current and past maintenance fees?

❖ If it is a right to use, how many years remain? Is it perpetual?

❖ Is there a secondary market?

❖ Where is the contract enforceable?

❖ Is it a timeshare or a travel club?

❖ Why is the owner selling it?

❖ Who are the legal owners, and do they all agree to sell the timeshare?

RIGHT TO USE WARNING

With a right-to-use timeshare or a travel club membership resale, you must obtain the documents that indicate when the contract expires. You don't want to purchase something that will expire in a year or two because the previous owner has used up many years. Most often, the ownership is good for thirty to ninety-nine years and may be renewable for a fee.

THE ALL-INCLUSIVE RESORTS

After working in the U.S., Mexico, and Canada for about thirteen years, I decided to work in the Dominican Republic. I had heard this was a great place to sell. Many Americans and Canadians were buying timeshares (travel clubs), and more companies were popping up to meet the growing demand.

When I arrived, it was not anything like I expected. I was totally unprepared. All the resorts were mandatory all-inclusive. Guests had no other options. In fact, there were no full kitchens like they had in the good ole days. There might be a small refrigerator for cold drinks. All-inclusive resorts include all meals and drinks, including alcoholic drinks, and activities for one flat fee.

As an experienced timeshare salesperson, part of my pitch was saving money with full kitchens. In the D.R., this was not to be. In fact, guests and timeshare exchangers had to fork out an additional $150 to $300 per day for their food and beverages, and it wasn't always the best quality food. THIS IS WHAT THE CHARGE AVERAGES WHEN THE GUEST ARRANGES AN ALL-INCLUSIVE PACKAGE. The term all-inclusive has a "free" ring to it, but families should decide if they will really eat and drink what the resort charges. They might be better off not booking an all-inclusive.

As a salesagent, my challenge was to figure out how they were so successful in selling timeshares when people had to fork out an extra $1,000 for their vacations, depending on how many guests there were per room.

Well, it didn't take long for me to figure this out. They were lying to the guests with more creativity than I had ever witnessed before.

If you're thinking about buying a beach-front property in these locations, inquire whether it is a mandatory all-inclusive resort. If it's not, it might be in the future, and you're stuck with it. Timeshare contracts are developer based. This means they can delete or reduce benefits at any time for pretty much any reason.

Unfortunately, most of the resorts in Cancun, Cabo San Lucas, Dominican Republic, and Jamaica have converted to mandatory all-inclusive resorts with no kitchen or the opportunity for guests to bring in their own food. In fact, they will not allow you to enter the resort unless you pay an additional "resort fee," even after you have paid your exchange fee and the mandatory all-inclusive plan. Do your research before investing in any of these properties. For some, the all-inclusive option might be ideal because you don't have to worry about your food and beverages, which are available all day and night.

All-Inclusive Plans Lack Flexibility for Dining Options

The all-inclusive package removes the flexibility of tasting the local cuisines, and sadly, the local restaurants cannot compete with the luxury resorts.

If the resort does not offer an alternative to all-inclusive, many guests are restricted to the resort's property. If you like eating at local restaurants and you're an adventurer or an explorer, it doesn't justify paying for the all-inclusive.

Although many of the resorts in Mexico and the Caribbean have a mandatory all-inclusive plan, some resorts do provide guests with the option of purchasing the all-inclusive program. Do your homework before booking or buying.

TRAVEL CLUBS ARE NOTHING BUT HOT AIR

When you buy a timeshare at one of the all-inclusive resorts, you don't own anything. You are buying air with no guarantees except that you must pay for their overpriced all-inclusive food and beverages on top of your maintenance fees if they have them.

Moreover, sales reps would tell the guests that they will receive discounts on airfare and other travel services to justify the costs. This is a lie. They do not get any more discounts than the person who owns nothing. I once heard a top salesperson in Mazatlán, Mexico, telling the guests that if they purchase that day, they will pay only $99 airfare from the U.S. to Mexico every year for life. Surprisingly, people believed this lie and bought it. That timeshare sales agent lives in a beautiful luxury waterfront home with a boat.

One of the new tactics of the mandatory all-inclusive resorts is to inform you that there are no maintenance fees. This is exactly what many timeshare owners are complaining about. This is untrue because the maintenance fees are built into the all-inclusive price. I worked at one resort in Jamaica where the average all-inclusive price, including the room, was about $500 to $700 per day for only two people!

THE TRAVELING CLUBS: THE NEWEST AND SMARTEST SCAM ON THE BLOCK

Now, there are traveling timeshare clubs that will contact timeshare owners or members, usually the elderly, and inform them that one of the exchange companies (RCI or I.I.) has an update for them. They will even offer to pay for their dinner at a local restaurant. This is another scam.

The company will purchase a list of timeshare owners in a specific demographic area. They will hire a call center to contact timeshare owners and inform them of the time and place for the meeting. During the meeting, they will offer to take away their timeshare and trade it in for another one that has a lower maintenance fee. Most of the time, this is a cash deal, or credit card accounts are opened to charge the purchase.

This tactic is nothing more than taking away one timeshare to purchase another. If there is no loan outstanding, the member's existing timeshares might have been deeded back to the resort. With these traveling clubs, there really is no guarantee.

The problem is that their original timeshare may not be traded in, so the owner finds themselves stuck with two timeshares and two maintenance fees. The company that sold them the timeshare is usually not from their state. Legal action can be cost prohibitive. Anyone in the U.S. victimized by this scam should file a complaint with the Better Business Bureau and the Attorney General of the state where you made the purchase. However, these overnight companies often change their names to avoid being included on online complaint sites or if they have logged too many *Better Business Bureau* complaints.

Some companies offer an array of accommodations all over the world, but the upfront cost does not guarantee anything. With these companies, you don't own anything. Some have no maintenance fees, taxes, or surprise assessments. The problem is that there is no security for the up-front costs. The company can fold the next day, and you will lose all your hard-earned cash with nothing to show for it. All they have to do is set up another company or LLC under a different name, and they are at it again.

I would not advise anyone to invest $4,000 or more for a traveling club membership—anywhere, anytime. Consumers should never buy a timeshare or travel club membership on the spot. Always conduct due diligence, regardless of how good the deal seems at the time.

As a former timeshare professional, I understand why resorts need to create urgency to make the sale the same day. In fact, "creating urgency" is a strategy employed by most industries, whether car dealers or clothing stores, that often display time-sensitive ads.

The adage, "out of sight, out of mind," is true. When guests are out of the high-pressure sales presentation and seriously consider their options in a calm environment, most will not buy. A timeshare can cost as much as a house, although the total purchase price increases gradually with each upgrade. Would you ever buy a primary residence if you always had to buy the house the same day you looked at it? If the resort offered a "today only" price, they should stick with it. Most will take the same price a day, month, or even a year later—whatever it takes to make the sale.

If resorts followed through with the promises made during the sales presentation, I believe more guests would purchase later. However, when they return home and begin to sift through the plethora of negative online complaints and reviews posted by others who purchased, they are more likely not to purchase later. If they did purchase while on vacation, then the reality of buyer's remorse sets in when they read the negative reviews. This justifies their right to cancel the deal with a full refund if they are within the contract rescission period. In the U.S., this period varies by state. Some states are as little as three days.

Conducting your due diligence is crucial when you are considering spending thousands of dollars for a timeshare or travel club membership. There are many out there with lots of options. Decide what you want and stick with that.

I suggest to consumers to NEVER buy a timeshare during a sales presentation at the resort. Use the sales agents as your guide to decide when, where, and how much you want to spend. Then, take it from there.

TOP TEN REASONS WHY AIRBNB IS BETTING THAN TIMESHARES

While working in the timeshare industry, a guest warned me that the timeshare industry should be concerned that Airbnb will take over and attract potential timeshare owners.

When he made this statement, at the time, I was working at the Villas del Palmar Resort in Cancun and was only concerned about making the sale. No, he didn't buy it.

Now that I have retired from the business, I have since evaluated what he said.

As a former timeshare sales and marketing executive who worked in the industry for over fifteen years, I agree that his statement is true on several levels.

In this consumer-driven digital age, there are some great deals on the internet: numerous travel agencies, websites, hotels, and bed and breakfasts. Airbnb is the new kid on the block that has developed into a multibillion-dollar online travel business.

Although Airbnb cannot compare to the high-end brand name timeshare resorts with gigantic pools and lots of kids' activities, there is something to say about a couple of guys who followed their dreams.

The company targets the millennial generation, as do the timeshare companies. For this generation, it's not always about the size of the room, the luxury of the hotel, or the full kitchen. It's more about the experience they can cherish for the rest of their lives.

Here Are the Top Ten Reasons Why Airbnb Is Better Than Timeshare

1. THERE ARE NO HIGH-PRESSURE SALES—JUST A WEBSITE!

Many consumers complain about the high-pressure timeshare sales presentations that are supposed to last for only ninety minutes but end up lasting over four hours.

The sales and marketing reps are friendly while luring consumers to attend a sales presentation and romancing them with all the amenities of the resorts. However, once you are in the salesroom, for many, it's often compared to being in prison. No matter how many times you say no and try to get away, they keep you there.

The sales reps in the timeshare industry are known for lying and being rude and mean to their guests once they realize they will not spend the $20,000 average asking price.

With Airbnb, all you have is a website. No marketing calls. No salespersons. No closer. Just a website. Simple. Easy.

2. THERE ARE NO LONG-TERM COMMITMENTS

With a timeshare, you must sign a long-term contract that commits you for life like a marriage. If you want a divorce, the other party may not be so understanding.

If you're not happy with your timeshare purchase, you are stuck with it, and nobody else wants to buy it. If you don't pay your maintenance fees or mortgage, timeshare companies will aggressively come after you like a dog after a bone. They can affect your credit and cause other financial and emotional difficulties.

If you choose not to go on vacation for one year, you are still committed to making the mortgage payments and the maintenance fees that continue to increase.

With Airbnb, there are no long-term commitments. There are no contracts to sign. You don't have to worry about the company ruining your credit or defaulting on you. If you choose not to go on vacation, you pay nothing because you are not obligated to do anything.

3. TOTAL TRANSPARENCY

When you own a timeshare, you don't always know what you're getting or what to expect after the initial purchase. After paying an enormous amount of money to these companies, you hope to at least get a room at the place in which you purchased. For many, this is not always the case.

The New York Attorney General settled with The Manhattan Club for $6.5 million in 2017 for what they called "false promises and shady sales tactics" to its 14,000 owners who could not make reservations at their home resort.

With timeshare, you hope they have a room should you decide to go on vacation at another location and must worry about exchanging your deed or points into something you hope is there. Your exchange power depends on what and where you purchased.

There are some places that many timeshare owners will never be able to exchange because of the high demand.

With Airbnb, there is total transparency. If you want to stay in an apartment in Paris, you can. You always know exactly what you're getting because it is right there in front of you. There is no guessing. It only depends on what you want to get, where you want to go, and how much you are willing to pay. You get to view the real photos of the rooms. You can look at other travel reviews and compare prices in the same areas.

4. SIZE DOES MATTER...IN SOME CASES

When you purchase a timeshare, the size of the room you get for your vacations depends on how much money you invested into the timeshare. If you don't own a high demand and low supply area, you might end up in a Motel 6-quality room. You never know what you're getting.

If you don't have enough points, you are limited, and you might not have enough points to stay an entire week.

With Airbnb, you know exactly what you're getting. It doesn't depend on a previous purchase but simply the location, type of accommodation, the size of the room you need, and how much you want to pay. Simple.

5. FEES

When you own a timeshare, you continually pay fees coming out of the woodwork.

You must pay the initial purchase price. If you took out a loan on the timeshare, you must pay the interest. For some resorts, their interest rate could be as high as 18 percent. Over time, you just bought yourself another timeshare.

You must pay the annual maintenance fees, which increase every year. Sometimes the timeshare companies do not maintain the property the way you expected. But you still must pay.

If you want to visit other places outside of the timeshare company's collection, you must pay annual membership dues to the exchange companies, which is about $300.

Additionally, you must pay an exchange fee each time you exchange. These fees are also about $300 per exchange.

Some resorts are now adding "resort fees," which were not mentioned when you purchased the timeshare. They average about $35 a day.

With Airbnb, everything is transparent. There might be cleaning fees and service fees, but you choose whether you want to pay or not.

6. YOU DEAL DIRECTLY WITH THE PROPERTY OWNER

When you purchase a timeshare, you will never see or speak to the salesperson again unless, of course, he is trying to sell you more timeshare. After the initial purchase, the owner must communicate with their customer service department, and sometimes they can be harsh.

If the company is not giving the owner what was promised in the sales presentation, they must deal with somebody who had nothing to do with the original sale. Even if the owner is not getting what was expected, they are still expected to pay their maintenance fees and mortgage. If they don't, beware.

If the owners have a problem through the exchange, they must contact the exchange company because the timeshare company has nothing to do with it.

With Airbnb, you can speak directly to Airbnb or the owner if you need to.

I had a personal experience I would like to share.

I booked an Airbnb for a trip to Van Nuys, California, for training. When I arrived at the apartment, there was cat poop everywhere. We contacted Airbnb. They asked us to send a photo. Immediately, they reimbursed our money. They paid for a night's hotel in another location and made the arrangements for another Airbnb nearby. Quick. Easy. No hassles.

7. NO AGGRESSIVE MARKETING REPS

When you are staying at a large timeshare resort property, they often see you as their next paycheck. They can't wait to get you on another high-pressure timeshare sales presentation or for an "owner's update" (same thing). They call your room, stop you in the blobby, and continue to hassle you throughout your vacation.

The original idea with the Airbnb plan was to meet others in a more intimate setting and make new friends.

If you even see the property owner, they will not hassle you with booking another night with them or returning. All they ask is a fair review on the website. It's your choice.

8. YOU ARE SUPPORTING LOCAL COMMUNITIES

Timeshare is now a $10 billion business that pays high commissions and profits to large companies, sales and marketing staff, and resorts. Everybody makes big bucks when consumers pay $20,000 or more for a timeshare.

At the all-inclusive timeshare resorts, often the members pay more than the public to stay in the same place. The money spent on timeshares goes to large companies, some with shareholders who want their dividend checks.

According to some reports, 89 percent of timeshare owners are dissatisfied with their purchase, and the timeshare companies are doing everything they can to continue to get their money. Some timeshare companies have hired law firms to help prevent timeshare owners from canceling.

If customers are dissatisfied after paying thousands of dollars for something that doesn't work, why should they stay in it?

With Airbnb, there are no worries. You are supporting local families like you and me. You are supporting local communities and mom-and-pop businesses that are just trying to generate some extra income. Airbnb takes only a small percentage of the fees.

Some families will become lifelong friends as you discover you have much in common.

9. THE PRICE IS MUCH CHEAPER WITH AIRBNB

The prices of timeshare have skyrocketed over the years, and so have the attached fees. If you add up all the costs of owning a timeshare, they could be astronomical. The problem is that current timeshare owners have no control. The timeshare companies can use any excuse they choose to raise prices, and owners have no say.

If a timeshare owner exchanged into another timeshare property, it costs much more in the long run. Otherwise, they're stuck with going to the same place every year.

Let's suppose a consumer purchased a timeshare and was expected to use it for twenty years.

Initial Purchase Price	$20,000
Annual Maintenance Fee	$900 X 20 Years = $18,000
Exchange Annual Membership	$300 X 20 Years = $6,000
Exchange Week	$300 X 20 years = $6,000

Total without inflation over twenty years is $50,000. With inflation, possibly double.

This is for a one-week vacation. If the timeshare owner used the resort's financing, the price would more than double.

Upgrades are a booming segment of the timeshare industry. They are getting timeshare owners to spend more money on more points.

With Airbnb, everything is your choice. If you want to stay in an entire apartment or home, you can choose to do so. The prices are right on the website.

I just looked up a beautiful apartment in Paris with an eighteenth-century Parisienne courtyard. The price was only $1,371 for the entire week for two people. I discovered many others for half that price. And this was last minute.

10. AIRBNB IS MORE ABOUT THE EXPERIENCE

Timeshares are generally located in high-demand tourist destinations often filled with crowded hotels, resorts, restaurants, beaches, and overpriced attractions. Although there are some timeshare resorts in more isolated locations, developers will not invest in those properties because it does not make financial sense.

With Airbnb, you can stay pretty much anywhere you want, and it doesn't matter to the folks at Airbnb because they don't have to build or own the properties.

The accommodation could be in crowded tourist areas if you desire. However, there are many accommodations in isolated areas where somebody is willing to rent out a room, apartment, house, houseboat, trailer, tree house, tent, or any other type of space in some of the remotest parts of the world. I can't wait for the inhabitants of the Amazon Forest to get a whiff of the Airbnb concept. It's not just about a place to lay your head at night but also about the experience.

Airbnb founders Joe Gebbia and Brian Chesky, two gentlemen who discovered and pursued their dreams, are nothing short of geniuses. Airbnb is now a $2.3 billion company, and it proves what Napoleon Hill's quote has impressed into the minds of millions of self-improvement followers: *"Whatever the mind of man can conceive and believe, it can achieve."*

For my money, I would rather stay in an Airbnb than a timeshare any day of the week. And now that I think about it—I can.

TIMESHARES VS. ONLINE TRAVEL SITES

Like Airbnb, online travel sites, such as Expedia and Travelocity, are quite competitive compared to timeshares or vacation clubs. For some of the same reasons why Airbnb is so much better, online travel sites can offer you competitive deals for all your travel needs.

Some sites, i.e., Kayak.com, will do the work for you and display a plethora of travel deals from a variety of websites, and you can choose the deal you desire. You simply provide your travel dates, destination, and other details, and their algorithm will do the work for you. Many of them will allow you to book without payment and provide an option to cancel within a certain period.

If you pay up front, others will also provide a full refund if you cancel within a certain timeframe prior to the reservation dates.

With timeshares and vacation club memberships, after your rescission period, you own them and are liable for a large amount of money.

HOW TO TRAVEL FOR FREE

If you are traveling with a group, most do not realize that they can generate a nice income from booking through a wholesale tour operator rather than a travel agency. Wholesale tour operators are how travel agents get paid. These tour operators will purchase a large portion of airline seats, hotel rooms, and other travel products and pay travel agents a 10 percent commission for their work.

Those who travel with groups have the same opportunity to earn a 10 percent commission for every ten tickets sold, or they will offer you one free travel package for every ten you book with them.

So, the next time you are traveling with a group, contact a wholesale tour operator or distributor and ask what they'll pay for your group.

CHAPTER 10

HOW THE POINTS
SYSTEM REALLY WORKS

POINTS ARE PURELY FOR PROFIT—BUT NOT YOURS

The points system came onto the scene somewhere around the late 1990s to early 2000s. The housing market was in a downturn. Aging resorts needed repair, and a growing number of original buyers that bought in the early '80s wanted out. As a solution, timeshare developers came up with the points-based timeshare. Converting weeks to points has been a boon for timeshare developers but often a bust for buyers.

I was working for Sunterra Resorts in Santa Fe, New Mexico. The idea of selling vacation points was something new and exciting. Sales agents started coercing deeded-week owners into giving up their fixed, deeded week in exchange for points. Newer point products tend not to be deeded. Foreclosing on non-deeded points is less rigorous than foreclosing on deeded real estate. Owners who agreed to convert had to pay $4,000 to $8,000 or more to convert, in addition to their original purchase price.

Moreover, when you book using points, the resorts and the exchange companies can make an additional profit from fees attached to the points. Some resort fees are as high as $59 per reservation, in addition to what you pay the exchange company to exchange the points. If you add up your initial purchase price, annual maintenance fee, resort exchange membership fee, special assessments, exchange company fee, and your point conversion fee, it rarely justifies buying points.

When you visit the resort where you bought the points and complain that you still cannot go where you want to, their answer is always, *"Well, you don't have enough points."* People continue to buy, despite availability complaints posted by even high loyalty-level members.

I have never been a fan of the points system. I am not convinced that buying points will get you more of what you want compared to owning a fixed or floating week. Sure, points are great for the developer, but for the consumer, in my opinion, you are simply paying for air. You have also lost control of what you previously owned.

Many points buyers are happy with their purchase. They find good value booking with points. For the timeshare developer, however, it is pure profit. There are satisfied point customers, but it's hard to ignore the volume of complaints found on the internet with many Attorneys General investigations (in the U.S.) and lawsuits galore.

POINTS OFFER SOME FLEXIBILITY, BUT FOR A PRICE

The sales agent will sell the concept of flexibility. The points member can break their one-week vacation into a shorter three-day vacation and save the remaining points for another vacation or getaway. This is attractive for members who do not or cannot travel for an entire week or would prefer to spend a few days at one resort and a few days at another.

If you own points in the U.S., the points are sometimes attached to a deeded property for a specific time, unit, and size, usually to a fixed-week timeshare unit and size. This will determine where and when you go. Supply and demand determine availability, not how many points you have. What fixed week you convert to points will also determine how many points you receive to use at certain resorts. Some resorts require more points.

The exchange companies know exactly what you own regardless of how many points you have. They know what week your points are attached to, and this is the information they must have to make your unit available to another exchanger.

Think about this: you cannot expect somebody with one thousand points in the Poconos Mountains to compete with somebody who owns one thousand points in New York City. It has everything to do with supply and demand, location, week, and the unit size attached to the points.

The Manhattan Club is a good example of how investing in points can end up as air. The New York Attorney General banned the owners of The Manhattan Club from working in the timeshare industry and fined the company over $6 million for limiting availability to those who purchased, while non-owners booking online could find availability. But the point (no pun intended) made earlier is location—New York City or Orlando? Which do you think has the highest value in the timeshare world?

Moreover, the resorts will tell you that you can have several short trips during the same week. This is highly unlikely, as it depends on availability. It is almost impossible to book three days in Paris, two days in Rome, and two days in London consecutively.

Flexibility comes with a price, and it may not be worth spending the extra dollars for the extra headaches that can plague the points buyer.

POINTS CANNOT GET YOU EVERYWHERE YOU WANT TO GO

While working for several resorts that offered points to existing owners and new owners, I became skeptical after learning that members could not find promised availability. When the member later complained about availability, the answer was always, *"They need to buy more points."*

If you view points as a currency, you are told they can be used anytime, anywhere. Well, that depends on where, when, what size, etc. Although the resorts talk about the positives of the flexibility of the points system, they don't tell you the negatives, which can make all the difference in getting where and when you want to go.

When you purchase points, you should receive a catalog or some type of schedule that explains the number of points needed to go to certain resorts. It also tells you the size of the unit and the time of the year you can travel with the number of points owned.

There will certainly be many places you cannot get into unless you have purchased a lot of points. This is frustrating for many timeshare owners because very few read the material. Even when the entire contract is read, the points buyer may still discover they were over promised availability after the rescission period has expired because they were not allowed access to the booking site until after the rescission period. The catalog shows the number of points required, but it will not show availability.

When you visit one of the resort properties, they will also try to sell you more points at a discount. Don't fall for the deceptive price freeze. Most timeshare points are worth pennies on the dollar, yet buyers often equate retail price with value. The sales agent will show the member a history of price increases but fails to mention the little to no secondary market. Eventually, you find yourself buying more points with an increase in maintenance fees, and you're back to where you started, still complaining about availability with less money in your pocket.

POINTS INFLATE OVER TIME

The most negative aspect to points timeshares, and timeshare in general, is the lack of a secondary market. Points have not increased in value, yet sales agents boast of price increases of 10 percent per year or more, waving their RETAIL price list and leading the consumer to think of the purchase as an investment. Never is the little to no secondary market discussed. Subprime mortgages and junk bonds had some value, but timeshare points are worth virtually nothing as soon as the buyer signs the contract if they need to sell them.

If you purchased points tied to a specific resort, you might have purchased ten thousand points to vacation at the same unit, size, and time every year. Five or ten years later, the points required may have increased to fifteen thousand or twenty thousand points. Now, you must buy more points to go to the same place. Some resorts will tell you that you don't have a choice. This is surely a lie.

Some resorts will state in their paperwork that the point requirements will remain the same. This is partially true. What they don't tell you is you may not have access to the new resorts unless you purchase more points.

When a resort brings on new properties, they often require more points to get into these new properties. If you want to get into the new resorts and stay for more than a few days, or at all, you need to buy more points, go off season, or stay in a smaller unit than you owned.

In my opinion, the points system is an intelligent business move for the timeshare developers but not for most timeshare owners coerced into forking out more cash for something they already own. Lawsuits have been filed by deeded owners who could no longer gain access to the unit, or sometimes even the resort, they had enjoyed staying at for years. Keep your deeded week. Usually, they cannot "legally" change anything you own unless there is a *mutual agreement by both parties*.

If you are considering purchasing points, check out the member-sponsored Facebook pages and websites in the resource section of this book before you buy, including TUG (Timeshare Users Group). Ask questions on these sites, and you will get honest opinions from some who are happy with their timeshare. Others will answer why they are not happy. I feel these groups are not industry influenced. Each is specific to a resort. It's good to get opinions from actual members and someone like me from the sales side of the transaction.

CHAPTER 11

THE MOST COMMON TIMESHARE AND VACATION CLUB COMPLAINTS AND HOW CONSUMERS ARE FIGHTING BACK

Why are there so many timeshares for sale? Why are so many timeshare owners or members even willing to give them away? There are a variety of reasons why so many timeshare owners want to dispose of their timeshares. These reasons can range from not being able to afford it any longer, a death in the family, or health reasons.

Of all the reasons I have heard, the following seem to be the most common reasons why many timeshare owners want to dispose of their timeshares:

❖ The sales and marketing agents used aggressive sales tactics. We felt we couldn't get out of the sales presentation unless we bought something.

❖ It doesn't work the way it was explained.

❖ We bought another timeshare at another location and no longer need two (or more).

❖ We don't need or want to use it anymore.

❖ The property is not kept up as we expected.

❖ The timeshare owner is deceased, and the family doesn't want it.

❖ We can't rent it out like they said we could.

❖ The maintenance fees are out of control.

❖ There are new resort fees that weren't there before.

❖ There is poor customer service.

❖ We don't feel we are getting what we paid for.

❖ We are not satisfied with the exchange properties.

❖ The exchange company won't provide what we want.

❖ There is never any availability at our home resort.

❖ There is no availability anywhere.

❖ We paid a timeshare relief (or resale) company money up front to get rid of our timeshare, but we still have it.

❖ We paid a timeshare listing company to list our timeshare, but we still own it.

❖ We traded in our timeshare for a new one but are still being billed maintenance fees for the old one.

There are many more complaints, but these represent the most common reasons why people want out of their timeshare.

Most timeshare contracts are perpetual. Given the limited to no secondary market, accompanied by rising lifetime maintenance fees, it's no wonder there are so many complaints. The deceived buyers may discover the deception only a day or month after the contract rescission period. Let's hope lawmakers and regulators wake up to the harm done to families stuck with this albatross.

U.S. STATE GOVERNMENTS ARE ASSISTING CONSUMERS

Some state Attorneys General in the United States have investigated and reached settlements with timeshare companies. An Attorney General does not act as your attorney, but if enough complaints are filed, they will launch an investigation that can result in a fine and an "assurance of discontinuance," meaning the company has agreed to stop fraudulent practices. It's rare for a company to admit its practices were fraudulent, but the company will agree to a settlement to make it go away.

The more consumer complaints, the more likely government and regulatory agencies will get involved. It is hoped more federal, and state regulatory agencies will take note to:

- ❖ help disgruntled consumers recoup some or all their money if deceived.

- ❖ enforce existing state and federal laws to protect consumers better.

- ❖ enact or strengthen laws to provide more disclosure.

- ❖ send out strong messages promoting consumer awareness, like the Federal Trade Commission's tips for timeshare buyers.

https://www.consumer.ftc.gov/articles/0073-timeshares-and-vacation-plans

The South Carolina Supreme Court ruled that dissatisfied timeshare owners can sue two Hilton Head Island timeshare companies. Some timeshare companies force arbitration. Many believe arbitration to be pro-industry. Arbitration is binding and

"The high court's opinion will allow the estimated 100 lawsuits that have been filed against two Hilton Head Island timeshare companies to go forward, said attorneys Joseph DuBois and Zach Naert, who represent timeshare buyers in the cases."

(Heffernan, 2017)

private, unlike a lawsuit because a lawsuit is a public filing. Some developers have a clause allowing the buyer to opt out of arbitration within a certain timeframe after the contract is signed. Buyers should do so.

Although the complaints should be decided by the state's real estate division, many complainants have been waiting for years for this unanimous decision.

If the state requires a real estate license to sell timeshare, then the salespeople and resorts fall under the state's real estate division. This is where dissatisfied owners can begin the complaint process. Some states only require their sales and marketing personnel to acquire a timeshare license. Lisa Ann Schreier, blogger and author of *Timeshare for Dummies,* provides a list of real estate requirements for timeshare sellers:

http://thetimesharecrusader.blogspot.com/2010/05/timeshare-license-information.html

WASHINGTON STATE ATTORNEY GENERAL WINS LAWSUIT

The Washington State Attorney General's Office settled with a company pocketing millions of dollars from innocent consumers by promising to get rid of their timeshares. According to the press release, the company promised to transfer people's unwanted timeshare to their own business without paying the underlying obligated or maintenance fees. The company claimed to have handled more than thirty

> *"The Attorney General's Office (AGO) has recovered $1.2 million from Jonathan Gibbs. This will cover full restitution for Washington state victims, between $1k-$20k, and all attorney's fees."*
>
> **(General, 2013)**

thousand such transfers from consumers within Washington state and nationwide.

DIAMOND RESORTS LOSES LAWSUIT

Diamond Resorts reached an $850,000 settlement and agreed to an assurance of discontinuance after hundreds filed consumer complaints with the Arizona Attorney General's office. The Attorney General's office helped Diamond owners get out of their agreements. Although Diamond did not admit any wrongdoing, the settlement speaks for itself.

I hope that Attorneys General in other states will consider taking similar actions against Diamond and other resort companies when members report a pattern of unfair and deceptive trade practices.

> *"The $800,000 settlement between the Diamond Resorts Corp. and the Arizona Attorney General's Office was reached earlier this year after hundreds of customers accused the corporation of using "deceptive sales practices" during time-share sales presentations, according to Mia Garcia, Attorney General's Office spokeswoman."*
>
> **(Frank, 2017)**

It is not uncommon for timeshare sales agents to make promises during the sales presentation that they know they can't deliver. Promises increase as high pressure builds in their effort to get a buyer to sign on the dotted line. Many companies state in their contracts that they will not guarantee anything unless it is specifically written in the contract. Mike Finn, of the Finn Law Group, has described this "oral representation" clause as "a license to lie."

This is from the Arizona A.G.'s Assurance of Discontinuance:

> *"Some of the alleged deceptions are related to the amount maintenance fees could increase annually, consumers' ability to resell timeshares to the public, the existence of Diamond buy-back programs, consumers' ability to rent out their timeshares for a profit, and discounts on other travel-related needs, Garcia (Arizona AG) said in a statement."*
>
> **(Frank, 2017)**

NEW YORK ATTORNEY GENERAL REACHES SETTLEMENT WITH MANHATTAN CLUB

The New York Attorney General's Office reached a $6.5 million settlement with the owners of The Manhattan Club timeshare project, one of the most expensive and luxurious timeshares in the country because of its prime location. Owners had complained for years that they couldn't use their own timeshares, while those booking online had easy availability. Also, the company wouldn't buy the timeshare back, as promised.

> *"The owners of the Manhattan Club lured thousands of timeshare buyers with false promises and shady sales tactics that violated New York law,"* Schneiderman said."
>
> **(Tacopino, 2017)**

131

WYNDHAM LOSES LAWSUIT TO WHISTLE BLOWER

A former Wyndham sales rep was awarded $20 million for wrongful termination. The company fired Trish Williams for exposing financial fraud to authorities. She filed a lawsuit and won.

> *"In 2010, the plaintiff, Williams, reported that elderly customers were being defrauded by Wyndham salespeople, who were opening and maxing out credit cards without their knowledge and lying about reducing interest rates, maintenance fees, and the ability to obtain rental income from their timeshares."*
>
> **(Firm, 2016)**

MARRIOTT VACATION CLUB POINTS SYSTEM QUESTIONED BY FLORIDA LEGISLATURE

Marriott Vacation Club's points system caught the attention of Florida legislators when they suspected that the company's points system may not be *in the best interest* of the timeshare owners.

> *"New York attorney Jeff Norton sued MVC last year, alleging in court documents that the company's entire sales structure is basically an illegal racketeering scheme because it uses a points-based system that was built on top of a system that previously sold deeds to real estate, among other things."*
>
> **(Paul Brinkmann, 2017)**

This Marriott lawsuit was ruled non-meritorious after Marriott worked to have an existing law amended to remove timeshare from the definition of beneficial interest. Attorneys for the plaintiffs felt this was an attempt to circumvent or out-legislate the lawsuit. The lawsuit said Marriott timeshare buyers "are being duped into believing they are obtaining title to a real-property interest ... when, in fact, they are merely getting a right-to-use license," the lawsuit says.

FTC PURSUES TIMESHARE SCAMMERS

The Federal Trade Commission (FTC) is cracking down on timeshare resale scams to help protect consumers from illegal practices but has not, as of the date of this publication, done anything to enforce consumer protection statute Section 5 regarding deception perpetrated by timeshare sales agents misrepresenting the product.

https://www.ftc.gov/about-ftc/what-we-do/enforcement-authority

The basic consumer protection statute enforced by the Commission is Section 5(a) of the FTC Act, which provides that **"unfair or deceptive acts or practices** *in or affecting commerce...are...declared unlawful." (15 U.S.C. Sec. 45(a)(1)).*

FTC Unfair Practices

An act or practice is unfair where it:

- causes or is likely to cause substantial injury to consumers.
- cannot be reasonably avoided by consumers; and
- is not outweighed by countervailing benefits to consumers or competition.

FTC Deceptive Practices

An act or practice is deceptive where:

- a representation, omission, or practice misleads, or is likely to mislead, the consumer.

- a consumer's interpretation of the representation, omission, or practice is considered reasonable under the circumstances; and

- the misleading representation, omission, or practice is material.

https://www.federalreserve.gov/boarddocs/supmanual/cch/ftca.pdf

As an increasing number of disgruntled timeshare owners file complaints with regulatory and law enforcement agencies, hopefully, investigations will lead to better enforcement of existing timeshare laws and the strengthening of disclosures. It would be nice to know the $100,000 timeshare you bought today will be worth nothing one day, after the contract rescission period, should you need to sell or learn you were duped into a purchase that fell short of what was promised.

> *"The Federal Trade Commission (FTC) and state agencies today announced a major takedown of timeshare property resale scams and phony or misleading travel prizes used to rope in unsuspecting consumers."*
>
> **(Lewis, 2013)**

FRUSTRATED CANADIAN TIMESHARE OWNERS LEGALLY SHUT DOWN WYNDHAM RESORT

According to an article on the Timeshare and Resort Developer Accountability (TARDA) website, frustrated timeshare owners of the Wyndham Carriage Ridge and Carriage Ridge Resorts in Ontario, Canada, legally shut down the resort to sell timeshares.

A survey conducted by the strategic accounting firm BDO determined that less than 13 percent of the owners wanted the resort to continue as a timeshare. Much of the frustration stemmed from aging timeshare owners who had no exit strategy to separate themselves from their timeshares when they could no longer travel and because of the lack of a secondary market.

Consequently, the homeowner's association threatened legal action against the owners and their heirs if they discontinued paying their maintenance fees. This move was causing already frustrated owners' financial hardships.

According to Karen Levins, who helped lead the actions against the resorts, court action resolved the issue by shutting down the resort to no longer operate as a timeshare.

"Today is a good day for democracy in Ontario. The results of the "exit/stay" vote demonstrate that CH and CR Owners will no longer have to live under the oppressive thumb of the timeshare industry's draconian practices. Under this Court-monitored process, an overwhelming number of CH and CR Timeshare Owners have clearly expressed their wishes to exit their timeshare relationship, and because of the landslide numbers, these two sister resorts will now be sold."

Karen Levin

U.S. VIRGIN ISLANDS BEING SUED FOR ADDITIONAL RESORT FEES

The U.S. Virgin Islands' government is being sued by timeshare owners because of the additional fees charged to use their timeshare.

> *"The fee is officially called the Environmental/Infrastructure Impact Fee, but it's not dedicated to the islands' degraded environment, such as its coral reefs, or crumbling infrastructure. Instead, most of it goes to the government's general fund."*
>
> **(Boiko-Weyrauch, 2017)**

The <u>American Resort Development Association</u> (ARDA), a Washington, D.C., non-profit organization for the timeshare industry, has filed a suit in federal court against the island's government for targeting non-resident tourists.

> *"the plaintiffs argue it is 'targeted, discriminatory, revenue legislation that has the purposeful intent to impose fees almost exclusively on interstate commerce violates the Commerce Clause,' citing various times Gov. Kenneth Mapp has said the legislation aims to seek funding from visitors to the territory."*
>
> **(Kossler, 2017)**

In addition to the timeshare companies, the exchange companies are coming under fire too for making promises they cannot keep.

RCI SUED.

RCI is being sued by five hundred British timeshare owners to recover millions of pounds. Although RCI cannot guarantee that one's timeshare could be exchanged anywhere in the world, this false promise is heard repeatedly during timeshare sales presentations.

> *"According to the claim — which could ultimately affect up to 9,000 British clients of RCI if the multi-party test case succeeds — the timeshare participants were rarely, if ever, able to exchange their right to use one property for an alternative holiday home of the same value in a different location."*
>
> **(Ames, 2016)**

RESORT OWNERS WIN THAILAND LAWSUIT

Thailand is protecting owners who purchased at the Laguna Holiday Club (LHC) in Phuket, Thailand. They did not get what they paid for, and it was very difficult, if not impossible, to book rooms. The owners filed separate complaints with the local consumer protection agency, and ten out of twelve were refunded their money.

> *"Most of the complaints are from LHC members who found it was very hard, or impossible, to get rooms from the Phuket Laguna group. Authorities claimed they had also acknowledged similar stories from foreigners who had made their complaints through embassies or online sources."*
>
> **(News, 2011)**

TIMESHARE ADVOCACY GROUPS HELPING TIMESHARE OWNERS FIGHT BACK

Disgruntled timeshare owners are fighting back and winning all over the world. Some groups are attracting the attention of regulators and legislators possessing the power to protect consumers from unethical timeshare practices. Others are getting loan cancellations and refunds for their purchases, while others are simply walking away. Sadly, for some, the outcome is foreclosure, as no one can guarantee a refund or loan cancellation.

Here are some timeshare user groups that are connecting frustrated timeshare owners with additional resources:

- Association of Vacation Owners
  https://avoworldwide.com/

- Timeshare Users Group https://tug2.net/

- Bluegreen Class Action Lawsuit
  https://www.facebook.com/groups/180578055325962/

- Timeshare Advocacy Group
  https://www.facebook.com/timeshareadvocategroup/

KNOW BEFORE YOU BUY

Before you purchase a timeshare, investigate the product and the company. Look at company reviews, good and bad, on *TripAdvisor*, Complaints Board, *Trust Pilot*, the *Better Business Bureau*, and other sites.

Bear in mind that the Better Business Bureau is a franchise community and does not rate the company. They merely rate how efficiently a company responds to complaints.

Some members have filed complaints complaining that the company called them asking them to call them back as the matter was time sensitive. When the member attempts to reach the company, there is no response. The company can report back to the BBB that they reached out to the consumer, but they did not respond. The BBB gives the company a gold star for reaching out!

Read the paperwork thoroughly before you sign anything but realize that there are many ways to be deceived that cannot be uncovered by reading the contract.

CHAPTER 12

HOW TO LEGALLY CANCEL YOUR UNWANTED TIMESHARE OR VACATION CLUB MEMBERSHIP

YOU CAN DISPOSE OF YOUR UNWANTED TIMESHARE

As mentioned earlier, there are many reasons why timeshare owners want to dispose of their timeshares. Too many sales agents and resorts have broken promises, and it is only fair that those who trusted them with their hard-earned dollars be able to depart civilly.

The question you should first ask yourself is, *"Why do I want to get rid of the timeshare?"* If the timeshare doesn't work the way it was explained, contact the resort to see whether you can resolve the matter amicably.

The reality is that many people of legal age sign contracts without reviewing them, especially the *terms of rescission*. Of the hundreds of owners that I sold to, only a few ever read the entire contract, including lawyers. To make matters worse, sales agents and resorts have ways of dodging the rescission period, as discussed in a prior chapter. Some things, like actual availability, cannot be determined by reading the contract.

Moreover, most of the contracts created recently separate the loan from the timeshare company. The contract will include a clause that the mortgage company is separate from the timeshare company. They are typically two different corporations. In other words, you agree that no matter what happens with the timeshare company, the mortgage must still be paid.

This would be like purchasing a car from a dealership, but the loan is with your local bank. The bank pays the dealership for the car. If the dealership decides to go out of business, does not service the car according to the agreement, or there are problems with the car, the loan must still be paid to the bank. Timeshare contracts are no different.

Even though you can get out of the timeshare, it has nothing to do with the mortgage you took out when you purchased the timeshare.

Getting out of a timeshare is like a girl breaking up with her boyfriend. After he has finally wooed her into dating him, the relationship takes a turn further down the road, and she wants out. Of course, his feelings are hurt because he doesn't want to lose her. He will make threats to her in hopes that she will return. But in the end, there is absolutely nothing he can do.

Likewise, there is very little a resort can and will do. Once payments stop, the resort begins with phone calls, followed by threatening letters. Check with the self-help resources listed in the resource section, like Timeshare Users Group, to find out what kind of repercussions others have experienced. The resort can damage your credit. In too many cases, the resort was the one who "breached" the agreement. They can't harm you physically. They can't take your job away. They can't separate you from your family and loved ones. They can't prevent you from enjoying life. They might foreclose on the property or try to ruin your credit, but in the end, that's all they can do.

You must decide what's more important: trying to fix something that doesn't want to be fixed or your mental and physical health.

TIMESHARE RESELLERS

If you are considering listing your timeshare on the resale market, I would suggest you list with an agency that does not charge you an upfront fee. Some companies charge thousands of dollars to list your timeshare, and there is no guarantee it will sell. Moreover, some will charge you annually regardless of whether it sells or not, and many are not licensed to sell timeshares. I would not suggest you list with these types of companies.

The LTRBA is a nationwide body of licensed real estate professionals dedicated to timeshare consumer protection and education. They offer professional representation for timeshare buyers and sellers, with no upfront fees. Adhering to the local, state, and federal laws are the hallmark of their commitment.

The Licensed Timeshare Resale Brokers Association and its members strive to provide ethical services to timeshare sellers and buyers in strict compliance with real estate law and the highest standards of full disclosure and fair dealing.

It is the real estate license that protects you, the consumer, and distinguishes them from the masses of non-licensed and non-regulated entities that have currently taken over the internet with exorbitant, non-refundable upfront fees.

The Licensed Timeshare Resale Brokers Association is an organization of licensed real estate professionals, who hold strong business ethics, and place the interest of the client before their own interests.

TIMESHARE ATTORNEYS

Given the litigious environment that exists at the time of this book's publication, we will not name specific law firms or lawyers we trust. Members should exhaust all avenues that exist by working with their resort, regulatory, and law enforcement channels before retaining an attorney.

Members can contact me through our website if they feel they need legal advice, and we will refer you to a law firm we trust. Be wary of firms, including law firms, with lofty-sounding names that include words like "consumer" and "advocacy," as the words may be applied opposite their meaning.

TIMESHARE CANCELLATION SERVICES

Many companies earn big bucks for legally getting timeshare owners out of their timeshares. Most, if not all, of these companies want money up front.

Many of these companies offer a money-back guarantee if they can't get you out, but the battle to obtain the money back can be as difficult as getting out of your timeshare. Obviously, getting rid of a timeshare with an outstanding loan is more difficult but doable, depending on the level of fraud. The reason for the money-back guarantee is that no one can guarantee they can get you out of your timeshare.

Many of these companies use creative scare tactics and warn timeshare owners that if they stop their maintenance fees, they will be in a lot of legal trouble. Often, they will run a projection of escalating maintenance fees over your lifetime, urging you to turn over the timeshare to them in exchange for whatever product they can make money on. Avoid "postcard" companies inviting you to attend a dinner to learn more about changes at your timeshare. They typically know little about your timeshare. This is just a come-on.

I have reviewed sites where major newspapers and attorneys provide inaccurate or incomplete information. I question their knowledge of how the industry works.

For example, the law offices of <u>Susan M. Budowski, LLC</u>, says on their website...

Get Rid of Your Timeshare - Legal Advice | Susan Budowski

Learn how to get **rid** *of a* **timeshare.** *You will not be able to get* **rid** *of your property until your* **timeshare** *is paid in full. Click to learn how to cancel it.*

The information posted on the website is irrelevant because not all timeshares are "timeshares." Many are travel clubs, like Costco, with no ownership and are located on foreign soil. Of course, she wants to get paid. She is called a "timeshare attorney." It is in no way true that you can't get out of a timeshare unless it is paid in full. It's not easy if you have a loan outstanding, but far from impossible. You don't hear about it because some companies require the member to sign a non-disclosure agreement, agreeing never to say anything disparaging about the company. Furthermore, many resorts are offering voluntary "deed-back" programs.

You can get out of a timeshare that's not fully paid if the contract has been breached by either party. We don't want to wade

146

into the waters of legal advice. We know of law firms that will offer an initial opinion without charge.

If a timeshare owner stops paying their maintenance fee, the timeshare company has a legal right to prevent them from using it. The same is true if the owner stopped making their monthly payments, did not follow the company's rules for reservations, renting, or destroyed the unit. The resort has a legal right to act against the owner.

Likewise, when the timeshare owner cannot use the timeshare as explained in the contract, the timeshare owners should have the right to act against the resort. If the owner follows all the rules and still cannot use their own timeshare, the contract has been breached. Proving it is usually an uphill battle, thanks to the oral representation clause, which states, "*I did not rely on oral representations to make my purchase.*"

To get rid of your unwanted timeshare, you simply need to know how to do it. There is much an owner or member can do on their own before contacting anyone who may charge to help you get out of the timeshare. Our taxes dollars pay for regulators and law enforcement agencies. Use them. If everyone just retains an attorney, the only thing that will improve is the attorneys' bank accounts. Filing regulatory complaints, as discussed previously, calls attention to unfair and deceptive business practices. The goal is reform.

Timeshare cancellation companies are making MILLIONS (as much as many resorts are making) by doing something that many timeshare owners can do themselves.

The timeshare industry is fighting back hard. It was announced at an ARDA conference that a $50 million fund had been set aside to put the crooks and the honest lawyers out of business. "We have your best interest at heart! Don't call an exit company!" warned one resort. Another launched a "scam buster" site. The company has over two thousand Better Business complaints filed against them. There are for sure some pots calling the kettle black.

We can't reproduce this link often enough—a thirteen-page, single-spaced listing of timeshare exit scams the Federal Trade Commission busted, working with the FBI and other agencies:

Some timeshare attorneys and sales reps for timeshare relief or solutions companies know very little, if anything, about the operations of the industry. They gladly pay administrative assistants or "intake" workers to fill in a template with your personal information so that an "assessment" or "evaluation" can begin. Most phone sales staff have never worked for or sold timeshare. They have been trained to answer questions to make the sale, including scare tactics.

Because of the phenomenal success of this sometimes legitimate, sometimes fraudulent cancellation market, timeshare companies are suing them because it cuts into their profits. It also interferes with their "inventory (that's you) recycle" program. An attorney or exit company will submit a "cease and desist" letter, meaning the resorts can't contact you for any reason, including collections calls. One resort reported that they have ninety collection agents making one hundred thousand calls a week! Members report being called twelve times a day, six to each spouse, even when the family struggles with medical issues. If you find yourself in this unfortunate situation, take some time to research fair debt collection laws.

In the end, if cancellation companies can cancel your timeshare, so can you. You just need to know how.

"Several timeshare companies have declared war on attorneys and businesses that advertise timeshare cancellation services."

(Paul Brinkman, 2017)

DISPOSING OF A TIMESHARE ON THE RESALE MARKET

Many timeshare owners can dispose of their timeshare without paying any fees, and in some cases, can get rid of it in a day. However, if you would rather list it on the resale market, the options are there.

The timeshare resale market is now a multibillion-dollar business because thousands of people want to dispose of their timeshares. Timeshare resale companies, attorneys, and real estate companies capitalize on this market by charging fees and making promises to get rid of them.

One timeshare resale company, Sell My TImeshare, lists more than fifty-five thousand timeshares for sale. They are making $77 million annually. They charge more than $1,400 just to list the timeshare on their site without guaranteeing that it can be sold. Timeshare owners must pay them annually to list their timeshares. They are not real estate licensed so by law cannot even advise a listing price or say, "The price is good." Too often, timeshares with no secondary market are listed. The already beleaguered timeshare member watches as the listing stagnates.

My advice is don't pay anyone up front to dispose of your unwanted timeshare.

There are many honest timeshare resale listing companies that operate with integrity and transparency. These companies will not accept money until the timeshare sale is complete, and they are licensed real estate agents. They are listed as <u>Licensed Timeshare Resale Brokers Association</u>. Their motto: *"Protecting Timeshare Consumers."*

CANCELLING WILL NOT AFFECT YOUR CREDIT SCORE

If your U.S. timeshare is fully paid off and doesn't have a mortgage attached, you have the power to cancel it without any negative impact on your credit score. That's right, folks - freedom from your timeshare is just a few simple steps away. Firstly, it frees up your financial resources, putting you in control of how you spend your hard-earned money. No more yearly maintenance fees, special assessments, or unexpected expenses draining your bank account.

Secondly, saying goodbye to your timeshare allows you to reclaim your precious vacation time. Instead of being limited to a specific location or timeframe, you'll have the flexibility to explore new destinations and experiences. Imagine the excitement of planning a trip without the restrictions of a timeshare schedule!

CONTRACTS CAN BE BROKEN

Under U.S. law, contracts can be canceled or terminated if either party does not fulfill the terms of the contract. They can be canceled because of fraud or a mistake. The problem is proving the fraud. Given the oral representation clause, when state regulators demand proof, the member is stuck.

There have been many Attorneys General investigations based on a high volume of complaints and the pattern of complaints. The Manhattan Club is a good example.

If you want to dispose of your timeshare and the resort has not fulfilled the terms of the contract, you can file suit against the resort with or without an attorney. Consider, though, that big-box developers have armies of lawyers. Filing your own lawsuit is probably the least desirable. There is much that can be accomplished via regulatory agencies and media outreach. Don't give up.

> *"Cancellation"* occurs when either party puts an end to the contract for breach by the other, and its effect is the same as that of 'termination' except that the cancelling party also retains any remedy for breach of the whole contract or any unperformed balance." *Uniform Commercial Code 2106(4); see 13 Corbin (Rev. ed.), §73.2; 13 Am.Jur.2d*

> ***"Termination"*** *occurs when either party, pursuant to a power created by agreement or by law, puts an end to the contract otherwise than for its breach. Uniform Commercial Code sec. 2106*

Sometimes the only remaining route is to ignore the resort and the collections calls. Allow them to spend the time and money to come after you. Most resorts will not go to court and chase you for a maintenance fee. They prefer to resell the property. It's best just to ignore them.

According to a *RedWeek* article, one of the attorneys in The Manhattan Club case mentioned earlier, Douglas Wasser, who represented the Manhattan Club owners, stated that he was not aware of any instances where the Manhattan Club filed any negative credit reports on its owners who stopped paying their maintenance fees. This legal action involved thousands of Manhattan Club owners who refused to pay their maintenance fees.

Timeshare companies, like anyone else, want to stay out of court. They simply want the legal right to resell the timeshare and generate another profit. It's all about money. It always has been and always will be.

TIMESHARE CANCELLATION COMPANIES VS. YOU

In my professional opinion, if the timeshare attorneys and the cancellation companies can guarantee to get you out of a timeshare, it is certainly something you can do yourself without paying anyone.

What concerns me is that the timeshare cancellation companies prey on innocent and beleaguered timeshare owners who see no other way out than to pay someone to get out. Many of these companies disguise themselves as "consumer advocates," pretending to represent the interest of timeshare owners when they are only after their money. The companies have nice-sounding names, but that doesn't necessarily mean it's a reputable company.

Some are in and out of business, change their business names, change owners, and take the consumers' money without getting rid of their timeshares. Some use several different business names, and others call themselves *consumer advocates* or *consumer credit agencies*, or their URL makes them appear as a nonprofit organization. When you search the internet, you end up at the same websites or offices. In the end, they are still timeshare cancellation companies.

Others guarantee that they can get rid of your timeshare. Some are successful, but why pay somebody for something that you can easily do yourself?

The Redweek.com timeshare forum conducted research on the repercussions of stopping payments and walking away from a timeshare. They even warn readers that resorts will use "aggressive" measures to go after timeshare owners who default on their timeshares. However, if you review the sources of this "research," they originate from resort owners, a resale company, or other entities that support the interests of the resort developers, including Wyndham, not the timeshare owner.

I am not going to call all timeshare exit companies scams. Nor will I say all sales agents and resorts employ

> *"...Lawyers rightly advise that this is a risky strategy, since you cannot control how the company will respond to your default. Some go after owners aggressively with collection efforts."*
>
> **(Redweek.com, 2016)**

deceptive sales practices. Disney Vacation Club is an example of a timeshare company with few complaints, backed up by satisfied owners.

Don't rely on celebrity endorsements, companies with great-sounding names, telephone solicitations, major network news, or print news media to provide accurate information about the timeshare industry. Beware of the "free consultation." It is nothing more than a sales pitch by a trained salesperson to gain your trust and get your credit card and personal information. When you sign up with one of these companies, you forfeit the right to even talk to your resort, as you have, in essence, turned over control by signing a power of attorney.

I recommend that you avoid all timeshare cancellation companies and timeshare attorneys and do the work yourself.

Whatever you do, NEVER pay an upfront cost. If you decide to pursue the timeshare cancellation company route or retain a timeshare attorney, make sure that your funds are held in an escrow account with a separate entity until the job is completed. Only do business ON YOUR TERMS. Remember, you've been down this road before.

According to these timeshare cancellation companies, they can get you out of a timeshare whether it is paid in full or not. There will be negotiations, but nothing is impossible.

The 10 Pitfalls of Hiring a Timeshare Cancellation Service

Timeshare cancellation services may seem like the silver bullet you've been waiting for but beware of the lurking villains—hidden fees and additional costs and other long term negative effects.

In this section, we will discuss the 10 pitfalls you should be aware of before investing in a timeshare cancellation service.

1.   HIDDEN FEES AND ADDITIONAL COSTS

Some cancellation services may have hidden fees that can significantly increase the overall cost of cancelling a timeshare. The first step in avoiding the hidden fees trap is to carefully read all the terms and conditions. Yes, it might feel like a tedious task, but trust us, it's worth it. Don't let those cunning fees hide in plain sight! When in doubt, never hesitate to ask the cancellation service about any potential additional costs. A reputable company will be transparent and provide you with a clear breakdown of all fees involved. Don't be shy—it's your hard-earned money we're talking about!

2. LACK OF TRANSPARENCY

Timeshare cancellation services might seem like the answer to your prayers, but beware! Some of these services operate in the shadows, leaving timeshare owners like yourself in the dark.

When it comes to timeshare cancellation services, understanding their processes can feel like cracking a secret code. Some companies choose to keep their methods shrouded in mystery, leaving you to wonder how they plan to release you from the clutches of your timeshare. It's no fun stumbling blindly through the cancellation process, yet some services conveniently skip over vital information. They fail to provide a comprehensive breakdown of the necessary steps, leaving you to guess what comes next. Transparency is the key to a successful timeshare cancellation journey. Reputable cancellation services understand the importance of providing clear information about their processes. They guide you through each step, ensuring you have a crystal-clear understanding of what to expect along the way. They openly share information about their team, credentials, success stories, and even potential challenges you may face. When choosing a cancellation service, prioritize those that prioritize clarity. Look for companies that provide comprehensive FAQs, accessible customer support, and clear explanations of their processes.

3. SOME SERVICES MAY TAKE AN EXTENDED PERIOD TO CANCEL YOUR TIMESHARE

Some timeshare cancellation services bite off more than they can chew. They underestimate the volume of cases they handle, leading to an overwhelmed staff and delayed processes. It's like waiting in line at a theme park during peak season, inching forward at a snail's pace. Timeshare cancellations involve navigating a labyrinth of legal intricacies. If a cancellation service lacks experienced legal expertise, they may find themselves entangled in endless loops of paperwork and legal hurdles. They may have a laid-back approach to their work, taking their sweet time with each case.

When engaging a timeshare cancellation service, it's essential to set realistic expectations. Understand that cancellations can take time, and unforeseen delays may arise. Prepare yourself mentally for the possibility of a lengthier process. Maintaining open lines of communication with your chosen cancellation service is crucial. Regularly check in, inquire about progress, and seek updates on your case. A gentle nudge here and there can remind them of your presence and keep things moving.

4. LIMITED SUCCESS RATES

Some timeshare cancellation services are masters of creative number crunching. They may inflate their success rates by cherry-picking the most favorable cases, conveniently omitting those that resulted in less desirable outcomes. Success rates alone provide little context regarding the complexity of cases handled. A service boasting a high success rate may have focused on simpler cancellations, while ignoring more challenging scenarios. Success can be subjective, varying from one individual to another. A cancellation service may define success differently than you do. They may consider a partial refund or a reduced liability as a success, while you seek complete termination of your timeshare agreement. They may use their high success rate as a marketing tool to lure in clients, but when it comes down to delivering results, they fall short.

A cancellation service that boasts a high success rate may struggle when confronted with complex legal challenges. They may lack the necessary expertise and resources to handle unique situations, leaving you disappointed. When selecting a timeshare cancellation service, don't solely rely on success rates.

5.   SCAMS AND FRAUDULENT SERVICES

Be cautious of unsolicited offers that come out of the blue. Scammers may contact you via phone, email, or even through social media, offering their services without you initiating the conversation. Legitimate services typically don't engage in such practices. Timeshare cancellation scams often dangle enticing promises of guaranteed results and immediate relief. They prey on your desperation, using persuasive tactics to convince you they hold the secret to your liberation.

One telltale sign of a timeshare cancellation scam is the demand for hefty upfront fees before any work is done. They may justify it as administrative costs or legal fees, but it's a red flag. Legitimate timeshare cancellation services typically charge fees upon successful completion. Scammers often lack the necessary credentials and legal expertise to handle timeshare cancellations. They may operate under false pretenses, using fake testimonials and misleading information to deceive unsuspecting victims.

6. POTENTIAL DAMAGE TO CREDIT SCORE

Let's be real – your credit score is like your financial fingerprint, and you want to keep it sparkly clean. But here's the catch: failing to meet your debt obligations with a timeshare cancellation service can have a ripple effect on that precious number. Your credit score may take a dip, waving goodbye to those dreamy interest rates and potential loans in the future. Talk about a real buzzkill! Ignoring your payment obligations to a timeshare cancellation service can have disastrous consequences for your financial reputation. When you neglect to make payments as agreed upon, it's like splattering a gloomy ink blot on your credit report. This stain can linger for years, impacting your ability to secure loans, get favorable interest rates, or even rent a new home. Yikes! Defaulting on payments to a timeshare cancellation service can trigger a series of unfortunate events. Your account may be sent to collections, resulting in relentless phone calls from debt collectors and a downward spiral of credit score destruction that's harder to escape than a labyrinth.

To protect yourself from a credit score disaster, make sure you're fully informed about your obligations to the timeshare cancellation service. Read the fine print, know your payment due dates, and stay organized like a well-prepared explorer charting their course.

7. LACK OF PERSONALIZATION

Imagine trying to fit into a one-size-fits-all outfit— uncomfortable, right? The same goes for timeshare cancellation services that employ a generic approach, disregarding the unique circumstances of each timeshare owner. Timeshare cancellation services that use a one-size-fits-all approach often fail to address the specific needs of each timeshare owner. They overlook crucial details that can significantly impact the cancellation process. Timeshare contracts and laws vary from one situation to another. An impersonal cancellation service may overlook important legal nuances that could affect the outcome of your case. Your financial circumstances play a vital role in the cancellation process. Generic cancellation services may not consider your specific financial situation, potentially leaving you with unexpected costs or missed opportunities for savings.

8. DISPUTES AND LITIGATION

You're seeking freedom from your timeshare nightmare, only to find yourself entangled in a web of disputes and legal battles. Unfortunately, dealing with unscrupulous timeshare cancellation services can lead to just that. Unscrupulous timeshare cancellation services often make grand promises they can't deliver. They may assure you of quick cancellations, guaranteed results, or even a full refund. However, when reality strikes, you find yourself left high and dry, with broken promises echoing in the distance.

Dealing with unscrupulous cancellation services can land you in the middle of unresolved legal disputes. They may mishandle your case, fail to follow proper legal procedures, or even provide incorrect advice, leading to prolonged battles and mounting frustration. Entrusting your timeshare cancellation to unscrupulous services can result in significant financial losses. They may charge exorbitant fees upfront, promising results they can't deliver. In the end, you're left with drained pockets and a sense of betrayal.

9. LIMITED CONTROL AND INVOLVEMENT

Imagine feeling like a passenger in your own timeshare cancellation journey, helplessly watching as expensive cancellation services take the wheel. Unfortunately, relying on these services can often lead to a loss of control and involvement in the process. Expensive timeshare cancellation services may prioritize their own agenda, leaving you with limited communication and updates.

When you rely on these services, you may find yourself in the dark, unaware of the steps being taken or the progress being made. You have valuable insights and knowledge about your timeshare, but expensive cancellation services may disregard your input. Expensive timeshare cancellation services often come with hefty price tags. They may charge exorbitant fees, leaving you with a drained bank account and limited control over your financial resources. When you relinquish control, you may miss out on valuable negotiation opportunities. You have a unique understanding of your timeshare and its value, and by being actively involved, you can explore potential options and pursue favorable outcomes.

Take the time to educate yourself about timeshare cancellation processes, laws, and your rights as a timeshare owner. Knowledge is power, and it empowers you to make informed decisions.

10. ARE YOU CONSIDERING SHELLING OUT MORE OF YOUR HARD-EARNED DOLLARS BY HIRING A TIMESHARE CANCELLATION SERVICE? SEEK ALTERNATIVES.

Are you considering shelling out big bucks for an expensive timeshare cancellation service? Well, we have good news for you! We're going to introduce the empowering world of DIY timeshare cancellation and online courses. Yes, you can take control of your timeshare destiny without breaking the bank.

With the abundance of information available online, you can educate yourself about timeshare contracts, legalities, and cancellation processes. DIY cancellation methods allow you to tailor your approach based on your specific timeshare and circumstances. You can develop a personalized plan that suits your needs and objectives.

One of the major advantages of DIY cancellation is the significant cost savings. You can avoid paying hefty fees to cancellation services and instead invest that money in other aspects of your life. Online courses offer the opportunity to learn from experienced professionals who specialize in timeshare cancellation. You can tap into their expertise and gain valuable insights to navigate the process successfully. These courses provide comprehensive learning materials, including video tutorials, guides, templates, and case studies. Timeshare cancellation courses offer flexibility in terms of when and where you study. You can learn at your own pace, fitting the lessons into your schedule without feeling rushed or overwhelmed.

When exploring DIY methods and online courses, conduct thorough research to find reputable sources. Read reviews, check testimonials, and ensure the materials align with your specific needs.

You might have fallen into one pitfall by purchasing a timeshare that you later regretted. Don't fall into another pitfall by engaging in the wrong timeshare cancellation service.

It's time to take charge and embark on your path to timeshare liberation!

UNLOCK YOUR FREEDOM: TIMESHARE CANCELLATION VIDEO COURSES

My groundbreaking video courses have been meticulously designed to empower timeshare owners like you with the knowledge and tools to legally liberate yourselves from the shackles of unwanted timeshares - without paying exorbitant fees.

Empowering timeshare owners at www.everythingabouttimeshares.com, I firmly believe that knowledge is the key to freedom. My courses have been carefully crafted to equip you with the step-by-step guidance necessary to legally cancel a U.S. timeshare that is paid in full or a Mexico or Caribbean timeshare, irrespective of its payment status. I understand the complexities of the timeshare landscape, and I have been committed to providing you with the knowledge you need to take control of your destiny.

My timeshare cancellation video courses break down the timeshare cancellation process into easily digestible modules. From understanding timeshare contracts to navigating legal intricacies, I leave no stone unturned in providing you with a comprehensive education.

With a whopping 220 students successfully completing my courses, none have returned dissatisfied. The results speak for themselves. You can be confident that you're investing in a program that delivers on its promises.

Imagine the joy of breaking free from the financial burden and constraints of a timeshare that no longer aligns with your dreams. Enrolling in my video courses is your first step toward reclaiming your life, your finances, and your future. Take charge of your destiny and liberate yourself from the grasp of unwanted timeshares.

I am dedicated to your success, and that's why I stand by my courses with a satisfaction guarantee. Should you encounter any difficulties along the way, I will be there to assist you at every turn. Don't wait another moment! Free yourself from the clutches of an unwanted timeshare today. Visit www.everythingabouttimeshares to enroll in my life-changing video courses and embrace a future unburdened by timeshare woes. Unlock your freedom now!

TIMESHARE CANCELLATION VIDEO COURSE STUDENT REVIEWS

Welcome to the inspiring section where our students take the spotlight! At Everything About Timeshares, I take immense pride in my mission to empower timeshare owners with the knowledge and tools to break free from unwanted timeshares.

I invite you to embark on a journey through the heartfelt experiences of those who have successfully completed our transformative video courses. In this section, you'll discover genuine and unfiltered reviews from my valued students who have taken the leap toward liberating themselves from the chains of timeshare ownership. These stories are more than just testimonials; they are powerful accounts of resilience, empowerment, and triumph over financial constraints.

As you read through the experiences shared by these students, you'll gain a deeper understanding of how my video courses have made a real difference in their lives. From navigating complex legalities to taking decisive steps toward cancellation, each testimonial showcases the life-changing impact of my timeshare cancellation video courses. Whether you're currently contemplating timeshare cancellation or have already embarked on your journey, these reviews will inspire and motivate you to seize control of your destiny.

I am immensely proud of the success achieved by my students and the newfound freedom they now enjoy. So, without further ado, let the stories of some of my elated students illuminate your path to a future unencumbered by timeshare burdens. Their words reflect the heart of my mission: to help you find your way to a life of financial liberation and personal empowerment.

I believe that the power to reclaim your freedom lies within you, and I'm honored to be part of your transformation. Join me as I celebrate the triumphs of my students and embark on a journey toward a brighter, more liberating tomorrow.

"I am so, so thankful for this course and Wayne's guidance. The Mexican timeshare had illegally given my info to a US collection agency who reported it to the credit bureaus, and it was flagged as derogatory and to remain on there for 7 years. With the info I learned here, I was able to have it removed in less than 30 days, and my credit score went back up to where it was prior to the derogatory account being reported."
 - Ami Yarbrough

"What I really needed to know was in lectures 13-16. However, everything in this course was 100% correct. He was right in how they deceive the consumer, use tactics and tricks to get the sale, and I was surprised to learn that legally they cannot take action against us because they aren't financial institutions and the vacation clubs don't even have licenses. This was super informative and I feel less stressed and more empowered. More importantly, I will never do this again. I am appreciative of Wayne sharing his knowledge to help the consumer win against these fraudulent Mexican vacation clubs." **- Wendy**

"I wish I would have had this course BEFORE going to Mexico!" **- Eric Baxter**

"Wayne Robinson is a former timeshare sales agent and executive who worked through Mexico and the Caribbean islands. He is an absolute expert in foreign bought timeshares." **- Irene Parker, Volunteer Timeshare Owner Advocate and Timeshare Blogger**

"YES! Done! This worked! better than I expected! The book and E-course provided a reliable pathway to achieve the kind of results I would not have achieved on my own. The eCourse and book are exactly what is needed to guide you out of a Mexico travel club and its maintenance fees! For a month, they did try collecting the maintenance fee or tried to get us to reinstate our program... (the calls have now stopped). Wayne's step-by-step guidance is easy to follow and gives useful advice. Along with the easy to adapt letters, made the process so much less stressful. It showed me how to stand my ground. Thank you so much Wayne for creating and sharing. A much-needed book & eCourse" - **Pamela Harrison.**

"Excellent course. I can't believe how easy it was to get out of my timeshare obligation. I spoke with several timeshare cancellation companies who quoted thousands of dollars to do what this course helped me to do in under 30 days. Everything that the instructor taught me in this course was 100% true. He also provided the documents I needed to cancel and how to reply to the resort after they receive the letter of cancellation. I recommend this course to anyone who wants to get out of their timeshare contract without affecting their credit rating. Thank you so much." - **Jolene Sue**

"Hello and thank you Wayne!!!! Completed the course almost a week ago. If I could give Wayne ten stars, I would!! Take the course !!!!!! It is all so worth it!!!!!!! Thank you again, Wayne." Regards, - **Marie Nilsson from Sweden**

"The course is well laid out and easy to understand. Wayne also included documents which you could edit according to your situation. If this wasn't enough, he also added a digital copy of his book, Everything About Timeshares. What I liked about the course was the concern Wayne has for his students. If you have a question or need something explained, Wayne follows up in a timely manner." - **Greg C.**

"This course provided me with an overview of what I wish I knew when I purchased a travel membership club in 2008. I was a single Mom that love to travel and thought this was a great investment for me and my kids. I made an emotional decision without being informed/educated. I appreciate Wayne C. Robinson for sharing his knowledge & educating those of us that have been victims of this scam of an industry. To exit a timeshare /Travel membership Club is terrifying as well. The exit timeshare companies are charging ridiculous fees to exit. Wayne provided the documents needed to exit. I had questions & he responded in a timely manner to assist me with the process. Today, I completed, notarized, and sent certified mail." - **Janice Butler**

"This course was perfect for my needs, and I am now empowered to cancel my timeshare deed without incurring high attorney's fees. A huge shout out to Wayne Robinson for putting this information together to help vulnerable consumers everywhere!" - **Celine Hermann**

"Thank you, Wayne, for putting together a plan to help be relieved of this Mexican vacation club contract. There is so much useless information out there on the internet. ...I took your course, and the information is helpful and gets me going in a direction." - **Mary Jo Pipkin**

CHAPTER 13

HOW TO GET THE MOST OUT OF A TIMESHARE OR VACATION CLUB MEMBERSHIP

TIMESHARES CAN BE A GOOD BARGAIN

Although timeshares, now vacation clubs, have gotten a bad rap, consider keeping it if you know how to use it. If you can't get out of it because of the debt, then keep it and use it. You bought it.

Whether you have a good deal or not, you own it. If you are not overburdened, why not enjoy it for the rest of your life rather than spend countless hours worrying about how you got screwed. There are worse things to complain about. Sometimes "making the best of it" works out better than you might think. There are probably as many positive as negative members for the timeshare you own.

I will show you the best way to use your timeshare and how you can travel all over the world staying in nice places. You don't have to worry about exchanging or any of the other hassles.

Fixed-week timeshares are probably the best option for many people if you have purchased them in a place where you would like to visit repeatedly. You know what you have. You know when you can go, and there should be no surprises. Enjoy the resort and have fun with your family.

FOCUS ON WHERE YOU CAN GO

Rather than focus on where you can't go, focus on where you can go. This could be more of an adventure than you realize.

There are other options for timeshare owners to travel the world, regardless of where you own. I guarantee that if you know how to use your timeshare, regardless of its location and season, there are many places you can explore. Sadly, many owners don't explore and become frustrated when the property they desire to exchange into is *unavailable*. What they don't consider are the available places. I find there are more than enough locations available for most families.

The couple I sold a timeshare complained that they couldn't get a week in Hawaii, which is one of the most difficult places to exchange into. They were adamant about exchanging into Hawaii. I contacted the couple and suggested Belize as an alternative, and they took my advice.

So, the opportunity to explore the world is available for the taking. You must review what is available when you want to go that is within your vacation budget. You might be thinking of taking a nice vacation to the Swiss Alps when availability is abundant in the Colorado or Canadian Rockies.

There are some places where there is always availability, regardless of the season or where you own.

Mexico is a great place for family vacations, and there is an abundance of availability in Cancun, Puerta Vallarta, and Cabo San Lucas. Florida always has availability. Parts of Europe, such as Spain or the Canary Islands, have lots of availability.

Also, you might consider vacationing during off or slightly off season. I exchanged into the Marriott's Village d'ile-de-France just outside of Paris for only $199 for a week in a two-bedroom townhouse through Interval International. Their nightly public rate was $300 per night at the time.

The key is to think outside the box and focus on where you CAN go.

Many timeshare owners get frustrated with their timeshares because they can't go where they want to go during the time they want to go. They get tired of the "no availability" excuse. Well, this should not be the primary reason to buy a timeshare—to go where and when you want. That is what *Expedia* and *Travelocity* are for.

Within the exchange company directories are hundreds of places that you can go that are readily available. When you deposit your week or points into the exchange company and provide the dates you want to travel, they will provide you with a list of places all over the world that are guaranteed available. The best way to see this is to go online. You DO NOT need to speak to a customer service rep.

Often, you will find units that are bigger than yours for the same exchange fee.

You might end up in the Swiss Alps in the summer in a two-bedroom suite. Think about it; you are in the Swiss Alps during the most beautiful time of the year. This could be an amazing vacation for you and your family. If you've got two weeks deposited, then stay there for another week or elsewhere close by. You've already paid for the airfare. Imagine two weeks in a two-bedroom suite in the Swiss Alps during the summer. What an amazing vacation. This is one of the hundreds of examples.

As I mentioned earlier, just because you want to take a vacation doesn't mean you must board a 747 jumbo jet and fly across the world. There are probably plenty of places you can visit that are within a day's driving distance.

Moreover, some timeshare owners would love to exchange their timeshare with you. TUG2.com provides a free service for members to exchange their timeshares with other owners.

HOW TO STRETCH YOUR DOLLARS

Most exchange companies have unused inventory under *Bonus Weeks, Getaways,* or *Last Call Weeks.* These weeks can often be purchased by members at a bargain. Even though you might have only one timeshare, you can use more weeks when you take advantage of these extra weeks that can cost $199 per week for a studio unit to $1,400 per week for a three-bedroom penthouse. Using these extra weeks can cut down on your total vacation costs because the more you vacation, the less it costs.

For example, if you exchange one week of your one-bedroom timeshare or points for somewhere else in the world, here is what you will pay, minus your initial purchase price. Let's suppose you spend a week at your home resort, and all you pay is the maintenance fee. If your maintenance fee is $800, your nightly rate is about $114 for a luxury suite. Not bad. If you compare that to a regular hotel suite, you might pay as much as $300 - $700 nightly, depending on the location and resort quality.

If you exchange your week, here is an example of what it will cost:

Annual maintenance fee	$800
Exchange company annual dues	$249
Exchange fee for one week	$249
Total	$1,298

Your total cost for accommodations anywhere in the world for a one-bedroom suite is $185 nightly. This is available anywhere within the exchange network for up to four people—a great bargain.

Let's say you want to purchase a bonus week or a getaway week from the exchange company, and the weekly rate is $249. That's all you pay. There is no additional maintenance fee, membership dues, or exchange fee. You just pay $249 for a one-, two-, or three-bedroom suite, depending on what they have available. Even if they give you only a studio or one-bedroom suite, your nightly rate is now only $36 for each suite, regardless of the size. You cannot get that rate at any hotel in the world for a luxury suite.

If you add up what you paid for both vacations, your average nightly rate is only $110 per night. The more bonus weeks you use, the less your overall annual vacation costs, even when you factor in your original purchase price. If you divide the cost over a thirty-year vacationing period, you're still getting a good value for your timeshare if you know how to use it.

The bonus weeks are available for a couple of reasons:

1. New resorts need to attract prospects. Timeshare owners who use bonus weeks might attend a sales presentation rather than those who do not own a timeshare. This results in a higher closing percentage. When you visit a resort, they will do all they can to get you to attend a presentation.

2. If a resort has an abundance of unused rooms, it is worth it for them to pay a small fee to attract guests through the exchange programs. In addition, guests will also spend

money at the bars, restaurants, excursions, and other services the hotel provides. Like they say, *"the most expensive hotel room is an empty one."*

TAKE ADVANTAGE OF PROMOTIONAL DEALS

Use the extra perks provided by the resorts. There are always new resorts that want to be a part of the timeshare industry. Hotels that want to generate more income may open some rooms specifically for timeshare use.

Look at the back of the exchange company magazines, and you will see the names of new resorts. They need to fill these rooms up with paying customers quickly. So, they will offer promotions for all timeshare owners to visit their resorts at a bargain. Some require you to take a timeshare presentation, but it is your choice to grab them or not.

Current owners represent the highest closing percentage in the business, and every resort loves RCI and I.I. owners who might buy another timeshare. If you go on the presentation and do not want to buy, at least get your gift, and if you have read this far in this book, you know exactly what to expect and how to take control. If you don't want to buy, tell them you are using the extra weeks, and they will always rush you through the presentation.

INVITE FAMILY AND FRIENDS TO HELP PAY THE COSTS

Have your family or friends pay for some of the airfare while you pay for the accommodations. This is a great way to vacation and costs less for you and them. You are on vacation in a beautiful location with the people you love, and they are paying for your airfare. This could cover your annual maintenance fee.

If you stay in a one-bedroom or two-bedroom suite, it's a good deal because everybody has more space. Sometimes, the exchange company will give you a larger unit if it is available without any additional costs. Most times, it is. Just tell them how many people you plan on taking. It doesn't hurt to ask.

EXTEND YOUR VACATION

While you're already on vacation, why not take a bonus week or a getaway and stay an additional week if you can get the time off. This is virtually having another vacation with free airfare anywhere in the world if you can find a timeshare week to stay in. If not, book a hotel or an Airbnb online to extend your vacation.

Book a getaway or bonus week for about $200 - $400. Sometimes, you can get one of these weeks in the same area or at the same resort where you are already staying. It doesn't hurt to try. Live a little and put some variety in your life.

There are many ways to stretch and enjoy your timeshare, regardless of where you purchased. If it's paid for and you've been trying to sell or get rid of it because it doesn't work the way you expected, you might reconsider keeping it unless, of course, you plan on burning all your luggage.

HOW TO RENT YOUR TIMESHARE

When considering renting out your timeshare, it must make financial sense. The questions you should ask yourself are:

- Why do you want to rent it out?

- Are you expecting to generate an additional income?

- Do you want somebody else to pay the maintenance fee?

- Do you feel you have no other options?

If you're renting out your timeshare just to offset your maintenance fees, it certainly is not a profitable move on your part. The most you may get out of it is paying one year's maintenance fees. This is something you will have to determine yourself.

There are many timeshares for rent all over the world, and most would be happy to have their maintenance fees paid but renting out a timeshare for a profit is something that must make financial sense.

Also, read the contracts. For example, Diamond Resorts does not allow renting via third-party websites like RedWeek. You can only rent to friends or family. Members have had their account suspended, issued a cease and desist, or terminated for renting, despite hundreds of ads displayed to rent. Check your resort rules before renting. Some resorts require the purchase of a guest certificate.

KOALA: ONLINE TIMESHARE MARKETPLACE

One option to rent out your timeshare is using KOALA, www.koala.vacations. The inception of KOALA traces back to a moment of insight experienced by Mike Kennedy during his tenure in the timeshare industry. As he interacted with timeshare owners facing the dilemma of unused properties coupled with burdensome annual fees, a unique concept took root. Being a timeshare owner himself, Mike envisioned a brilliant solution: a platform that could seamlessly connect these owners with vacationers seeking affordable accommodations, ultimately leading to a mutually beneficial arrangement for all parties involved – a true win-win situation.

Driven by this vision, Mike Kennedy joined forces with James Burbridge, a technology entrepreneur, and together, they embarked on the journey to co-found KOALA. Their mission is clear: to bridge the gap between timeshare owners and potential vacationers, while revolutionizing the timeshare industry with principles of transparency and fair play.

Their website: www.koala.vacations

Calculate Your Financial Risks

If you want to generate an income from renting your timeshare, like any other financial structure, you must weigh the costs.

- ❖ Original purchase price
- ❖ Annual maintenance fee
- ❖ Agency or listing fee (if there is one)
- ❖ Resort transfer fee (if there is one)
- ❖ Advertising
- ❖ The possibility of an assessment should the unit be damaged by the renters

Unless you have a fully paid timeshare with low maintenance fees and your resort is in high demand, then it's highly unlikely that you'll become Warren Buffet overnight. In fact, most likely, you'll lose money in the long run.

However, for some busy families, renting out their timeshare may be a means of offsetting costs until they have the time to vacation in later years.

If you decide to rent out your timeshare, make sure you use an organization that will make your ad visible to as many people as possible to generate lots of traffic to their site.

USING A TIMESHARE RENTAL AGENT

Many timeshare owners will use a timeshare listing agency that specializes in vacation rentals. Some owners are successfully renting out their timeshare. Some agencies charge an upfront fee to list your timeshare, and there are no guarantees it will be rented on time. I wouldn't use them unless I had a guarantee.

Renting probably works best with deeded week timeshares. They often take their commissions once the rental income comes in and send you the remainder.

KOALA is transforming the timeshare industry with transparency and fair play. They have built an online marketplace that connects vacation travelers to timeshare owners. With KOALA, these two communities connect and transact safely and securely. KOALA charges owners a modest commission, ranging from 8 percent to 10 percent, for help with booking and payments. KOALA vacation subscribers can earn travel credits to use towards bookings and members-only concierge services. The cost is $99.99 per year or $9.99 per month, and membership can be canceled at any time.

The prices you see on Koala include all booking fees, including resort fees. Nothing hidden, no surprises. Visit their website: https://www.go-koala.com/.

There are many companies that specialize in renting timeshares, and vacationers often look at these sites when considering rental options.

VRBO (HomeAway) has been around for many years, helping timeshare and other vacation owners rent out their properties. The service fee is between 6 percent to 12 percent of the rental cost. They have a slick website (www.vrbo.com) that displays all the property details.

TUG2.com – This is a timeshare users group that lists timeshares for sale and rentals for free with a $15 annual membership fee. You can place up to twenty-five ads per year with your membership. (https://tug2.com/timeshare-classifieds)

Redweek.com is a timeshare users group that has three options for renting, which range from $29.99 - $79.99.

Sellmytimeshare.com is the largest timeshare internet sales site that handles rentals. However, they do not disclose their fees online, and you must speak to a specialist to get a quote. I would be suspicious of anyone who doesn't advertise their fees. (www.sellmytimesharenow.com)

Airbnb seems to be the newcomer on the block when it comes to timeshare rentals. Timeshare owners are using this service to rent out their timeshares.

Unfortunately, Airbnb has more support for the renters than the owners. If you have a floating week or a points-based timeshare and your renters decide to change their mind after you have confirmed a reservation, you must work with the resort to change the time, and you must pay for any additional charges or fees. If you have a fixed week timeshare, this makes it easier and more convenient.

RUN A CLASSIFIED AD

Some timeshare owners successfully rent out their timeshares by running an ad in a local newspaper, Craigslist.org, Angieslist.com, online shopping centers, or their church or community center for a nominal fee or for free.

If you have a Facebook or Whatsapp group, you might post your timeshare unit for rent, and social media has many features to help you promote anything you want.

Whenever you can, obtain photos or videos of the interior and exterior of the property so that renters will know exactly what to expect. Show the front entrance, the lobby, the suite, the pool, the gym, and photos of the surrounding areas. Provide them with the local activities for families or any other attractions in the area. Pretend that you're the travel agent, and woo them with your ad.

During my fifteen years in the business, I have met people who own up to eighteen timeshares, and they usually use them. If they don't use them all in one year, they will rent them out to pay for that year's maintenance fee or give it away to family or friends.

Some people are preparing for retirement, so they rent it out until they retire. Then they can use it whenever they want, as they have more flexible schedules. Rather than request a specific week or property, they most likely see what is available and make their vacation plans around that.

If you rent it out simply because you no longer vacation and want to offset the maintenance fees, you might consider selling it or giving it up.

Keep in mind that should anything happen to the property, you might be responsible for any additional costs incurred from damages or theft unless the renters take responsibility with their credit card companies. Ask the resort.

Rather than using up all your energy trying to figure out how to get rid of your unwanted timeshare, determine whether it is best to use it to explore the world.

CHAPTER 14

THE TIMESHARE AND VACATION CLUB CAREER ENVIRONMENT

I worked in the vacation club profession for more than fifteen years and have listened to thousands of single men, women, and couples from around the world express an interest in changing their lives if only they had the opportunity. Some have bluntly confessed, "*I wish I had your job.*"

Most vacation club professionals work part-time, some seasonally, which allows plenty of time to pursue one's heart's desire.

> "*Some of the people in timeshare are in it for the fun, others for the money, and some for the adventure, and some for all of the above. I have met doctors, bank managers, entrepreneurs, paediatricians, soldiers, carpenters, landlords, biologists, airline pilots, the list goes on, who are working in some heavenly places selling timeshare for a living.*"
>
> **(First Glimpse of the Future, 2009)**

Here are the job descriptions of vacation club professionals available worldwide:

SALES

T.O./Closer Sales Rep

Until a salesperson has enough experience in this arena, they will probably have a more experienced vacation club salesperson or manager help close the deal. They are responsible for getting the credit card. There are certain popular terms for each of these positions. The person who closes the sale is called a "T.O." (take over), closer, or manager. Once the closer comes to the table, the salesperson introduces the couple. Depending on the company's policy, they may or may not remain at the table. If a salesperson does remain at the table, they must keep silent. Depending on the company's policies, some closers will share their commission. The salesperson who does it all is called a "front to backer." They can generate up to $20,000 monthly, depending on their sales volume. I have known some who have generated up to $30,000 in one month.

Assistant Sales Manager

The responsibility of the assistant sales manager is usually to close deals and assist others in closing deals. He works directly under the sales manager and will usually roam the salesroom to help answer questions and handle objections. They can generate up to $20,000 monthly, depending on their sales volume.

Sales Manager

Sales managers run the salesroom and work directly under the sales director, project manager, or developer and are responsible for helping the company reach its monthly goals or budget. Sales managers are generally paid a commission from overall sales and are responsible for training, hiring, firing, motivating, and informing liners and front to backers (a sales rep who performs the duties of a liner and a closer). They sometimes set rules and regulations to create a smooth, harmonious, and productive environment for the sales team. They are the day-to-day managers and can generate over $20,000 monthly, depending on their sales volume.

Sales Director

The sales director works directly under the project manager or developer. They coordinate with the sales and marketing managers to ensure a smooth transition, from inviting a stranger to a sales presentation to making a sale. They are responsible for meeting the company's scheduled financial goals. They make big bucks for attending meetings and overlooking resort sales. They must apply their experience, judgment, and power to produce sales. This high-profile position generally provides a very comfortable income, depending on the property size and sales volume. They can generate $50,000 or more monthly, depending on their sales volume. Some are millionaires.

MARKETING

OPC Manager

The OPC (off property contact) manager works with the developer or sales director to bring in the tours. They are responsible for hiring, firing, and training the OPCs. This position requires strong management skills. Many OPC managers have been promoted from OPC positions because of their strong sales figures. You've got to start somewhere. They can generate over $20,000 monthly, depending on their sales volume.

OPC REP

An OPC is the person who invites guests to attend a timeshare presentation. If they are not on the phone, they are in hotels, airports, or other tourist areas. Their job is to convince prospects to attend a sales presentation, and they use a variety of gifts to lure them. They typically receive a small bonus for bringing in guests and commissions on sales.

ADMINISTRATION/CONTRACTS

VLO (Verification Loan Officer)

The responsibility of the verification loan officer is to review and sign purchase documents with the new clients in accordance with local laws. A reputable company will assure that the VLO cleans up any misrepresentation (heat) or misunderstanding regarding the product and what the product can and cannot do. Sometimes the closer will do the paperwork, but this is usually performed by an outside person who was not involved in the sales process.

The paperwork usually includes a purchase agreement, loan contract, declaration, rules and regulations, maintenance fees, and anything else related to the usage and ownership of the property. Some VLOs earn a salary, while others get a commission. Some get both. At one resort where I worked, the VLOs generated about $8,000 monthly.

Project Director

The project director is responsible for the day-to-day operations of the resort property. This would include sales, marketing, operations, and building the resort if it is a new property. Many have come from the ranks of the sales and marketing teams and worked their way up. This is a high-profile position requiring knowledge of all aspects of building and operating a resort project. They can generate well over $50,000 monthly, depending on their sales volume.

NON-SALES AND MARKETING STAFF

Non-sales and marketing staff who work within the U.S. must be paid a salary, depending on the position, for at least minimum wage.

For staff who work at timeshare resorts outside of the U.S. and Canada, most often, the salary is poor and is usually much less than minimum wage in undeveloped countries. In the Caribbean and Mexico, the staff often earn $300 - $400 monthly. I have spoken to staff required to work extra hours without any pay at all. In these third-world countries, there is little they can do because there are no strong labor laws to protect them.

Most of the staff are uneducated and lack the communication skills to become sales or marketing agents targeting educated Americans and Canadians. Besides, most are satisfied with the security of a regular salary, and the straight commission structure does not appeal to them.

BONUSES

If the sales and marketing agents reach a certain volume in sales, there is usually a cash reward bonus. This is usually another 1 percent to 3 percent in additional commission, depending on the sales volume of the previous month.

CLOSING COSTS

The new purchaser must pay closing costs, which is another form of commission. Closing costs can range anywhere from $499 to over $2,000, depending on the resort. However, new owners are told that the charge is for legal documents and attorney's fees. They add this to the down payment to assure that they receive that extra commission up front, the key to their negotiations. The closing costs are usually divided up between the sales and marketing management team after paying the exchange enrollment and other minor legal documents.

CHAPTER 15

IN THE NEWS: THE TIMESHARE GAME - THE PLAYERS, THE MOVES, AND THE POLITICS

The timeshare industry has become a game. Over the past twenty years, there have been more players, more private equity investors, and more politicians getting involved in this multibillion-dollar industry. The industry is facing backlash from timeshare members tired of being deceived into purchasing, tired of some state regulators walking lockstep with the developers echoing, "You signed a contract" despite the FBI and attorneys arguing the oral representation clause does not allow over-reliance on it.

Informed consumers are communicating, thanks to social media, so unfair and deceptive sales practices, as defined by the Federal Trade Commission in the U.S., are being acted upon. Eventually, states that respond with an auto-denial, "You have no proof" letter will be brought to task. There are too many people aware of the deception that has been ingrained for years. Just as #metoo protests sexual harassment, allowing the abnormal to become the norm is not healthy for individuals or industries.

The rules of the game are changing as the industry struggles with social media, which allows owners to compare stories of deception. The only new laws regarding timeshare have been prompted by powerful timeshare lobbyists, like the Florida bill passed in 2015, making it more difficult to get out of a timeshare contract due to "nonmaterial" errors.

Timeshare wars continue as timeshare developers sue anyone attempting to help beleaguered members be released from contracts. Many timeshare buyers claim they signed because of unfair and deceptive sales practices.

To catch up, the timeshare industry is revising its marketing strategies, rewriting its contracts, setting up illegal offshore corporations, buying up other timeshares, suing timeshare cancellation companies, and wooing politicians to remain in their corner.

THE NEW TARGET MARKET

Timeshare companies have always used effective marketing campaigns to lure consumers into timeshare sales presentations. These marketing gimmicks typically involved free vacations, excursions, and sometimes cash. Historically, they target the elderly residing in certain zip codes.

Millennials and minorities seem to be the new target market for the timeshare industry. This seems to be the same market that Airbnb is targeting.

According to a survey conducted by Dr. Amy Gregory of the University of Central Florida's hospitality management department, the timeshare industry has a pristine image with this inexperienced generation. Some students stated that they had "some familiarity" with timeshare and have visited a timeshare property. Of all the dimensions rated in the survey, the three highest ratings considered "valuable" were new experiences, luxury, and pampering.

In another article, Dr. Gregory describes the millennial generation as the next target, "larger and more influential" than any previous generation, including the baby boomers.

Timeshare resorts will lure this group into a timeshare presentation, romance them with luxury, and bark to them that "they deserve it." If the sales team is convinced, they cannot afford the timeshare, they will do all they can to make it easy and simple for them to get involved—TODAY.

Most resorts will do this by spreading the down payment up to six months. For many millennials and minorities, this makes it much easier for them to say yes and sign the paperwork. Once the full down payment is made, then the low monthly payments (but high timeshare interest rates) could last up to ten years.

This group needs to be aware that the company they are getting the loan from is not the same timeshare company doing the presentation but a separate mortgage company set up by the timeshare company. Unknowingly, they are agreeing to an unsecured mortgage loan. By doing this, the contract with the timeshare company is separate from the mortgage. If the timeshare owner is dissatisfied with the timeshare, the mortgage payment must continue, regardless.

Some developers do maintain the contract. The worst thing a borrower can do is transfer the loan to a third-party lender. On the surface, this sounds logical due to the high timeshare loan interest rate, but transferring, say to a home equity loan, means your dispute with the timeshare company now requires a refund rather than a loan cancellation. Stopping payments will bring the timeshare company to the table if they ignore your complaint, but if the loan is transferred to a third-party lender, the member is now asking for a refund as opposed to a loan cancellation, a more difficult negotiation.

This leaves little, if any, protection for the consumer should the company not live up to what was presented during the sales presentation, files for bankruptcy, or simply goes out of business, as was the case with the Friar Tuck timeshare resort in Catskills, New York, and other properties.

Maintenance fees tend to increase annually, so think about rising maintenance fees over the lifetime of a younger buyer.

Additionally, few buying a timeshare realize there is little to no secondary market for timeshare. Would you buy a boat, car, condo, or home that you could not sell? Again, check out the secondary market to see if you can avoid that initial outlay, especially if you are financing at 12 to 20 percent. The market is flooded with people who want to get out of their timeshare. Timeshare companies list this as a risk (to their shareholders) in their annual reports, in essence admitting they are restricting the secondary market.

I suggest millennials and minorities stay away from the timeshare game and go with Airbnb. No contract. No hassles. No games.

NEW MEMBERS ARE SADLY OFTEN MISLED

I recently received an email from a recent Wyndham buyer asking me to help him cancel his timeshare purchase. During the sales presentation, he asked the sales representative to show him the member website. The salesperson's response was that the new members would not have access until two weeks after they purchased.

During the sales presentation, the sales rep showed him the locations that he could travel to throughout Asia and the number of resorts that would be available. Once he finally did have access to the website, the availability mentioned during the sales presentation was non-existent. He decided to cancel his membership.

As a new Wyndham owner, he signed a contract that stated he agreed to pay off the mortgage of $47,000, regardless of whether his timeshare worked or not.

Do not sign anything until everything you want, or was promised, IS IN WRITING. Otherwise, do not buy. The buyer should ask the sales agent to show them in the contract where ANY claims made by the sales agent appear. A common ploy is for the sales agent to say, "This has not been made public yet, so don't say anything to the QA person."

UPGRADES HELP KEEP TIMESHARE COMPANIES AFLOAT

According to some reports, 46 to 70 percent of new timeshare business is developed by owner upgrades. This "cash cow" has developed over the years, first by "coercing" deeded owners to convert to points, and secondly, hard selling current owners to purchase more points. A common complaint voiced by existing members is that they were told buying more points or upgrading to the next loyalty level would allow them to sell points or pay maintenance fees, but the programs turned out to be nonexistent.

Upgrades have become a big market to help the industry remain afloat. This market depends solely on current timeshare owners who are sometimes tricked, lied to, and misled into buying more points, tantamount to purchasing another timeshare.

Timeshares companies send their best sales reps to work in their "in-house" sales team. This group of handpicked sales reps is specifically trained to coerce current owners into investing more money during their owner "updates." The owner updates are opportunities for the company to generate more sales from sometimes already frustrated members.

The answer to any problem that the owner has is always, "*you need to buy more points.*" Whether the issue is availability, exchanging, quality, or size of the room, the answer is always, "*you need to buy more points.*" The sales rep will offer more points at a discount, more free trips (that are not free), and more RCI weeks (worthless) and tell them they can now go anywhere anytime with their improved program—after you sign on the dotted line and give us your credit card.

There have been many complaints lately due to the prevalence of electronic signing. It's shocking how many times I've heard members were not aware a credit card in their name was opened and charged. Some did not even know they bought a timeshare until they got home and received correspondence.

iPads and tablets are difficult to read, your initials are stored, and you tap, tap, tap your way into insolvency. One family did not know until they got home that they had purchased $142,000 in additional points and had $17,000 charged on a new credit card. They were told they were signing up for a new loyalty program, and the credit card would help them pay maintenance fees. A common trick is to ask the prospect to fill out an application to determine if they are qualified. If they qualify, the person is often never informed that the card was opened and charged.

The sales agent tells the buyer they have offered them a deal that they cannot refuse, and many do not refuse. It's bad enough that members were coerced into trading in their deeded timeshares to a points system, but now they are pressuring current owners into buying more points.

TIMESHARE EXCHANGERS CONVERT INTO HIGHER SALES

Resorts will designate a special team for incoming timeshare owners exchanging into their resort from another resort through one of the exchange companies.

These exchangers, for many resorts, convert into a high volume of sales, so they will do all they can to earn their business. They are already familiar with the concept. The exchange obviously worked. Most likely, they have exchanged from an older property into a nice, more appealing property. And they can trade in their old timeshares for a new one to get equity back.

In my opinion, this is trading one problem for another. No timeshare company gives anything for a trade-in, period.

OWNER'S BEWARE OF THE HILTON GRAND VACATIONS AND DIAMOND RESORTS ACQUISITIONS

In 2021, the news of Hilton Grand Vacations' acquisition of Diamond Resorts reverberated through the timeshare industry. With a staggering $1.4 billion deal, the merger brought together a colossal force, boasting 710,000 owners, 48 sales centers, and over 20 new markets. Undoubtedly, HGV anticipated significant value creation from this newfound scale. However, as a seasoned expert in the timeshare realm, I urge owners to be cautious of potential tactics that may be employed during such mergers to "upgrade" their existing ownership.

Timeshare mergers often bring excitement to owners, who eagerly anticipate gaining access to new resorts through the partnership. It's not uncommon for companies to dangle the allure of "upgrades" during mandatory owner updates, presenting them as blessings that enhance the owner's experience. But here's the reality that owners should be aware of: these seemingly attractive upgrades can come at a steep price, sometimes matching or even exceeding the original investment in the timeshare.

While the prospect of accessing new resorts may seem enticing, it's essential for owners to thoroughly review the fine print and consider the implications of upgrading their timeshares to these supposed "better opportunities, i.e., HGV Max." The truth is that owner upgrades represent a significant portion of the timeshare industry's profits, accounting for up to 50%. As such, it's crucial for owners to exercise due diligence and avoid falling into potential traps.

During timeshare mergers or acquisitions, companies may strategically use the allure of new resorts and exclusive membership benefits to encourage owners to "upgrade" their existing membership or purchase an entirely new HGV membership. These tactics can lead to additional financial commitments that may not align with owners' original intentions or budget.

As a trusted expert, I advise timeshare owners to approach such offers with caution and to thoroughly assess the costs, benefits, and long-term implications of any upgrade. Don't be swayed solely by promises of enhanced experiences; instead, focus on aligning your timeshare decisions with your individual needs and financial goals.

While the merger between Hilton Grand Vacations and Diamond Resorts undoubtedly holds potential, owners must be vigilant and informed about the choices they make. As the timeshare industry continues to evolve, education and awareness remain paramount for owners to make informed decisions and protect their interests.

Remember, the success of any timeshare experience lies in a well-informed owner who understands the nuances of the industry. By staying informed and carefully evaluating upgrade opportunities, timeshare owners can navigate the waters of a merger and make choices that truly benefit them in the long run.

BEWARE OF TIMESHARE SCAMS: PROTECTING YOURSELF FROM FRAUDULENT SCHEMES

Timeshare owners nationwide are falling victim to cunning scams, resulting in losses of millions of dollars. In 2022 alone, the FBI Internet Crime Complaint Center (IC3) received more than 600 complaints, totaling approximately $39.6 million in losses from individuals targeted by scammers regarding timeshares owned in Mexico.

The modus operandi of these scams has persisted for years. Unsuspecting timeshare owners receive unexpected phone calls or emails from individuals masquerading as sales representatives from reputed timeshare resale companies. Employing high-pressure tactics, these representatives create a sense of urgency, coercing timeshare owners into agreeing to sell their properties. However, the catch lies in an upfront fee requirement, allegedly covering listing, advertising, and closing costs. Once the fee is paid, the company becomes evasive, with unanswered calls, disconnected numbers, and inaccessible websites, or they concoct additional fees, stalling the real estate transaction indefinitely.

To exacerbate matters, some timeshare owners, already defrauded by the sales scam, are approached by fraudulent timeshare recovery companies. These individuals promise assistance in recovering lost funds but demand upfront fees for their services. In some instances, scammers pose as government entities, requesting payments for alleged fees linked to the timeshare sale.

To shield yourself from these scams, consider these valuable tips:

- Exercise caution when receiving uninvited calls, texts, or emails from individuals expressing interest in your timeshare.

- Thoroughly research all entities you interact with. Independently verify their authenticity by contacting their offices directly and seek assistance from a trustworthy real estate agent or lawyer.

- Be wary of high-pressure sales tactics and time-sensitive offers.

- Remember that offers that seem "too good to be true" often prove to be just that.

REPORT IT: If you or someone you know has fallen prey to a timeshare-related scam, promptly file a complaint with the IC3 at www.ic3.gov. Ensure to provide any available information, such as email addresses, phone numbers, company names, and details about the interaction with the scammers, even if no funds were lost in the process. Vigilance and swift action can play a pivotal role in combating these fraudulent schemes and protecting yourself and others from becoming victims of timeshare scams.

WHAT HAPPENED TO THE TIMESHARE EXIT TEAM?

Less than half a year after Washington State Attorney General Bob Ferguson made a public announcement, Reed Hein & Associates, also known as the Timeshare Exit Team, has been ordered to cease its deceptive timeshare exit practices and shell out $2.61 million to the state. Moreover, the company could face an additional penalty of $19 million if it breaches the terms of the consent decree. As a result, the company has now officially closed its doors, yet another example of unscrupulous third-party exit companies leaving consumers in a lurch.

It's disheartening to see this pattern of timeshare exit companies resorting to fraud and deceit just to make a quick profit, only to vanish when they fail to live up to their grandiose and too-good-to-be-true promises. The fallout leaves thousands of consumers paying the price for their dishonest actions.

In July of the same year, the Better Business Bureau reported that Timeshare Termination Team, a company known for abrupt door-closings, had ceased all operations without any prior warning. Their website is now inactive, and countless consumer inquiries regarding upfront fees that yielded no value remain unanswered. Speculations abound that the company may have filed for bankruptcy.

This is not an isolated incident. In 2019, American Consumer Credit faced severe consequences, being ordered to pay a staggering $23 million in civil penalties. The company was permanently barred from engaging in any future exit activities. Around the same time, American Resource Management Group also declared bankruptcy with $20 million in consumer creditor claims outstanding. The group faced multiple lawsuits linked to deceptive practices and false advertising. Interestingly, the group operated under several other business names, and the bankruptcy list included Redemption and Release, Resort Exit Team, Resort Release, and Vacation Properties for Less.

Back in 2018, the Castle Law Group, another timeshare exit business, faced harsh repercussions when its founding attorney was disbarred by the Supreme Court of Tennessee. The charges were manifold and centered around consumer fraud complaints, eventually leading to the shutdown of the business.

These stories serve as cautionary tales, highlighting the need for vigilance when dealing with third-party exit companies in the timeshare industry. Consumers must exercise discernment and thoroughly research any company promising to terminate their timeshares. It's essential to protect oneself from falling victim to deceitful practices, leaving behind a trail of shattered dreams and financial loss.

DAVE RAMSEY, CHRISTIAN RADIO HOST, CONFRONTS $150 MILLION LAWSUIT ALLEGING FRAUDULENT TIMESHARE EXIT COMPANY PROMOTION

Christian radio host Dave Ramsey finds himself entangled in a legal battle as listeners bring forth a monumental $150 million lawsuit. Allegations claim that the listeners were deceived by a timeshare exit company that Ramsey promoted on his show.

In the wake of this legal confrontation, Ramsey's reputation faces scrutiny as the lawsuit accuses him of endorsing a timeshare exit company that purportedly engaged in fraudulent practices. Listeners claim that they were led to believe in the company's promises, only to be left defrauded and financially burdened.

The lawsuit sheds light on the complexities of the timeshare exit industry, raising concerns about the responsibility of media personalities and influencers when endorsing such companies. As the case unfolds, it may prompt broader discussions on the need for transparency and accountability in product promotions, especially in sensitive financial matters like timeshares.

For Ramsey, a prominent figure in the Christian radio sphere, the lawsuit poses a significant challenge, putting his credibility and reputation on the line. As the legal proceedings progress, the outcome will be closely watched, with potential ramifications for the wider media landscape and the promotion of financial services.

THE BAD NEWS FOR THE TIMESHARE SECONDARY MARKET

The resale market has certainly cut into the profits of timeshare companies, as there is a plethora of timeshares for sale on numerous websites. Smart consumers are visiting these sites for bargains they cannot get from the resort. Timeshare resale sites are popping up all over the internet, and real estate agents have become savvy about this source of income.

However, the timeshare industry is pulling another trick to remain afloat. Most contracts state that the resort must agree to transfer any timeshare from a current owner to another, and the seller must pay a hefty transfer fee, as is the case with Diamond Resorts. Diamond requires a secondary market buyer to buy half the points they purchased on the secondary market to be a member of The Club, the internal exchange program. To our knowledge, Diamond is the only major timeshare member of the Licensed Timeshare Broker Association that they will not accept a listing for because they believe Diamond's secondary market restrictions are draconian.

Many resorts are not recognizing the resold timeshare unless the new owner purchases more points. This move is the perfect setup for yet another sale by informing secondary market buyers, "*You need to buy more points.*" The resorts are putting into the new contracts that the transfer does not include "ancillary rights," the rights or benefits given to the original owner. To receive full benefits, the new owner must purchase more points. Some of these points are into the tens of thousands of dollars. Basically, they are purchasing another timeshare.

This secondary market destruction could prove a shot in the foot for the timeshare industry. Can you imagine what would happen to the primary residential real estate market if the home you purchased had no secondary market? Or that a home with a loan could not be easily resold? New contracts are mentioning that "there may not be a secondary market, as the points do not appreciate." This has not stopped some sales agents from selling timeshare points as an investment.

Consumers are becoming more aware of unsavory tactics, which is why there are so many timeshares for sale that just sit there. The resale sites are generating millions in profits. Listing agencies that charge money upfront, unlike licensed brokers, care little that the $1,500 or more charged for a listing will stagnate.

My advice for dissatisfied timeshare owners who want to get rid of their timeshares—walk away.

WHERE ARE THE BIG THREE WHEN IT COMES TO TRANSPARENCY?

The powerful but low-key players of the timeshare industry, regarding transparency, are the two largest timeshare exchange companies, Resorts Condominiums International (RCI) and Interval International (I.I.) and the timeshare lobby, American Resort Development Association (ARDA). These organizations represent millions of timeshare owners and should be responsible for protecting the interests of both the developers and the consumers with full transparency and integrity.

While ARDA does fight for owners when the issue affects both the industry and the member, when the issue is at odds, like better disclosure, ARDA invests millions in fighting the consumer. Advocacy groups were outraged after ARDA worked to pass the 2015 Florida law making it more difficult to get out of timeshare contracts due to nonmaterial errors.

Timeshare consumers are fighting back. Quebec passed Bill 178 in 2018, redefining timeshares as a service contract with liberal avenues for cancellation, like services not living up to what was promised.

The exchange companies service millions of members worldwide who pay annual dues and additional fees to exchange their timeshare for another location. For most timeshare owners, RCI and I.I. are the only exchange options available.

On ARDA's website, one of the ways they "*promote the growth and development*" of the industry is by acting as an advocate for all the players involved. Members are billed $3 to $10 per contract on their maintenance fee invoice if the timeshare is purchased in America. It's called a "voluntary" donation to ARDA ROC. Few owners know what ARDA ROC stands for yet collectively give this organization $5 million a year in "opt-in" or "opt-out" contributions. Take time to research what ARDA ROC does and does not do before contributing.

> "Actively involved in local, state, and national governmental affairs, ARDA monitors regulatory issues that affect timeshare. ARDA engages in lobbying efforts focused on the establishment of a legislative environment that fosters industry growth and further enhances consumer confidence and protection."
>
> **(AARD.org, n.d.)**

When it comes to "further consumer growth," their efforts seem to lean towards the developers rather than the consumer.

According to an article written by Jeff Weir of *Redweek*, Dr. Amy Gregory, assistant professor at the University of Central Florida who teaches timeshare-related courses, stated at an ARDA convention that 85 percent of timeshare owners are dissatisfied with their timeshare purchase. If this is the case, how are the Big Three improving "customer confidence and protection?"

Regarding travel clubs, why aren't the Big Three transparent and admit that many resorts are not owned by the timeshare companies listed on their sites? Most of them rent rooms and own nothing, giving members the impression that they might have a chance to vacation there. Why don't the Big Three require travel clubs to have business licenses to sell timeshares?

If it weren't for the timeshare owners who pay their mandatory fees, all of them would be out of business, including the timeshare companies. If they were genuinely concerned about the timeshare owners, why don't the Big Three demand that resorts be more transparent to "*foster industry growth and further enhance consumer confidence and protection,*" as ARDA mentions?

ARDA's *Discovery* magazine calls itself "*the voice of the timeshare industry.*" So, ARDA, where are the voices of the consumers? The slick digital publication focuses more on educating the developers on becoming more "innovative" in their sales and marketing strategies. Nothing is said about becoming more innovative towards customer satisfaction.

ARDA's annual conferences are more like an Amway convention for the timeshare developers who pat each other on the pack for a job well done. When reviewing their schedule for their 2018 Caesar's Palace Las Vegas convention, there was no owner representation.

> "*This dark side of the travel club industry has increasingly produced criticism by marketplace advocates and law enforcement alike. However, as recent marketing campaigns suggest, this scheme is as popular as ever.*"
>
> **(David Beasley, 2013)**

I challenge the Big Three to man up and discover more "innovative" ways to represent the consumer rather than the timeshare developers.

THE SQUEAKY WHEEL GETS THE MOST ATTENTION

Most complaints that come my way are from Diamond Resorts, Bluegreen Resorts, Wyndham Resorts, and the Mexican and Caribbean travel clubs. Yes, many others could be included, but these three keep coming up. On the flip side, Disney Vacation Club has few complaints.

I would love to see more Attorneys General offices take action against companies that seem to encourage and reward deception. Some of these agents are earning more than $1 million a year selling timeshare points.

From reading timeshare advocacy reports, the Nevada Real Estate Division (NRED) and the Florida Timeshare Division, DBPR, appear to be supporting timeshare developers over consumers. The Nevada Real Estate Division typically responds that owners need proof before they can take their complaints seriously. It is legal in Nevada to record an in-person meeting without the other party being aware. It is not in Florida. So, what proof could a buyer even obtain in Florida?

As a licensed Nevada timeshare salesperson, I heard the lies. The resorts can be quite creative.

The squeaky wheels always get the most attention. If you feel you experienced unfair and deceptive sales practices, file regulatory and, if needed, law enforcement complaints. Join advocacy Facebook groups; reach out to lawmakers and the media. In some states, the court of public opinion is the only court open to the consumer.

I would suggest that consumers stay away from the three timeshare companies mentioned above and the travel clubs, where there is little protection or recourse, regardless of which state or country the timeshare is purchased. I recommend NOT buying a timeshare product in Nevada or Florida. In my opinion, many of these resorts are cunning and unethical, and so are the lawyers who draw up the contracts.

Lawmakers, local and federal government agencies, and the Big Three should be looking after the interests of the consumer, not just the interest of the developers.

Before you sign anything relating to a timeshare or travel club membership, demand the time that you need to read the contract and all the documents thoroughly. Demand that promises made during the presentation are available for viewing before the rescission period. Have the contract reviewed by an attorney. Make sure you know exactly what you are doing.

If they will not provide a copy of the contract for you to review without giving a deposit, simply walk away.

I challenge my readers to find their own thirteen shocking secrets you learned from reading *Everything About Timeshares.* I asked Irene to come up with her secrets. Here's her list and let me know what you have discovered. I would love to hear from you!

EXPLORE THE FASCINATING WORLD OF TIMESHARES ON "EVERYTHING ABOUT TIMESHARES" YOUTUBE CHANNEL!

Are you curious about the ins and outs of the timeshare industry? Do you want to stay informed about the latest trends and developments in this captivating realm? Look no further than the "Everything About Timeshares" YouTube channel!

Welcome to my engaging and informative platform, where we delve deep into everything related to timeshares. As a passionate expert in the field, I am committed to sharing valuable insights, debunking myths, and providing you with the most up-to-date information on the ever-evolving timeshare landscape.

What to Expect on "Everything About Timeshares": Exclusive Video Content: Our YouTube channel brings you exclusive video content, offering an immersive experience like no other to keep you engaged and informed.

Unraveling Industry Secrets: Timeshares can be complex, but fear not! We make it our mission to unravel the industry's secrets, simplifying intricate concepts, and providing you with a clearer understanding of how timeshares work.

Latest Trends and Updates: Stay ahead of the curve with our channel's timely updates on the latest trends, news, and developments in the timeshare sphere. Whether it's changes in regulations, emerging travel destinations, or innovative ownership models, we've got you covered!

Interactive Community: Join our vibrant community of timeshare enthusiasts, where you can share your thoughts, ask questions, and engage in lively discussions. Your feedback and insights are invaluable in shaping our future content!

Empowerment and Protection: As an advocate for consumers, I am dedicated to empowering you with knowledge to make informed decisions about timeshares. By staying informed, you can protect yourself from potential pitfalls and make the most of your timeshare journey. Don't miss out on the opportunity to explore the captivating world of timeshares with us!

Subscribe to "Everything About Timeshares" on YouTube and hit that notification bell to stay updated with our latest videos.

Whether you're a seasoned timeshare owner or a curious newcomer, our channel has something valuable for everyone.

Remember, knowledge is power, and together, we can navigate the timeshare industry with confidence and excitement. Join us on "Everything About Timeshares," where we bring you the expertise, passion, and camaraderie you've been looking for. See you there!

REFERENCES

AARD.org. (n.d.). "Who We Are." http://www.arda.org/who-we-are/whoweare/overview.aspx.

Adams, S. 2017. "Growing Demand For Timeshare In India." RCT Ventures, October 26, 2017. https://rciventures.com/news/india/growing-demand-timeshare-india/.

AFIA, E. P. 2015. "State of The Vacation Timeshare Industry - United States Study." Washington, DC: ARDA International Foundation.

Amy Gregory, T. K. (2014, April/May). A Glimpse Into Millenials Perception of TImeshare. Developments Magazine 34-37. Retrieved from http://www.nxtbook.com/ygsreprints/ARDA/g40308_arda_aprmay2014/index.php#/36

Ames, J. 2016. "Hundreds Sue Timeshare Club in 'Swap Scam'." The Times, May 9, 2016. https://www.thetimes.co.uk/article/hundreds-sue-timeshare-club-for-swap-scam-lbrsf8srb

Bizjournal. (2003, September 29). ILX Resorts facing lawsuit . Retrieved from Bizjournal: ILX Resorts facing lawsuit

217

Boiko-Weyrauch, A. 2017. "Timeshare Owners Are Suing the U.S. Virgin Islands Over New Fee. Marketplace, August 4, 2017. https://www.marketplace.org/2017/08/04/economy/timeshare-owners-are-suing-us-virgin-islands-over-new-fees.

Daskal, L. 2016. "Four Scientific Reasons Vacations Are Good for Your Health." Wikimedia Commons, June 13, 2016. https://www.inc.com/lolly-daskal/4-scientific-reasons-why-vacation-is-awesome-for-you.html.

David Beasley, D. O. 2013. "Travel Club Scheme: Inside the Promotion Commotion - Investigative Summary." Better Business BureauApril 2013. https://www.bbb.org/us/storage/50/documents/Travel%20Club%20Schemes%204-25-13.pdf.

Firm, D. L. 2016. "$20 Million Verdict for Wrongfully Terminated Whistleblower." Dolan Law Firm, November 18, 2016. https://dolanlawfirm.com/2016/11/wyndham-vacation-whistleblower-verdict/.

Foundation, A. I. 2018. "Timeshare Sales Increased for the Eight Straight Year!" ARDA Timeshare Datashare, June 2018.

Frank, B. J. 2017. "Arizona Settlement Releases Timeshare Owners from Contracts with Diamond Resorts." AG Central, May 7, 2017. https://www.azcentral.com/story/news/local/arizona/2017/05/18/timeshare-holders-released-contracts-following-deceptive-sales-practices/329107001/.

General, W. S. 2013. "AG Bob Ferguson Announces Settlement of Major Timeshare Scam Case." Washington State Office of Attorney General, September 12, 2013. http://www.atg.wa.gov/news/news-releases/ag-bob-ferguson-announces-settlement-major-timeshare-scam-case.

Goldstein, D. 2016. "Six Things to Know Before You Buy a Timeshare." MarketWatch, October 31, 2016. https://www.marketwatch.com/story/6-things-to-know-before-you-buy-a-timeshare-2015-02-17.

Heffernan, E. 2017. "Angry Timeshare Buyers Can Now Sue Developers, SC Supreme Court Says." The Island Packet, May 18, 2017. http://www.islandpacket.com/news/business/article151110492.html.

Insider, T. (2017, February 1). $1billion Law Suit against Diamond Resorts International! Retrieved from Timeshare Insider: http://www.insidetimeshare.com/1billion-law-suit-diamond-resorts-international/

Kossler, B. 2017. "Timeshare Group Suing Over Timeshare Fee." The Source, May 2, 2017. https://stthomassource.com/content/2017/05/02/timeshare-group-suing-over-timeshare-fee-2/.

Lewis, T. 2013. "FTC Cracks Down on Timeshare Resale, Travel Scams. Feds and States Launch Takedown of Schemes; 184 Face Criminal Prosecution." Consumer Affairs, June 6, 2013. https://www.consumeraffairs.com/timeshare-news-and-scams.

Marks, T. (2016, February 23). Consumer Repoerts. Retrieved from The Timeshare Comes of Age: These vacation ownership arrangements are attracting younger, more educated, more affluent buyers, thanks to consumer-friendly changes in the industry — but risks remain: https://www.consumerreports.org/travel/the-timeshare-comes-of-age/

News, T. P. 2011. "Laguna Timeshare Counter Complaints." The Phuket News, November 23, 2011. https://www.thephuketnews.com/laguna-timeshare-counters-complaints-27705.php#8DL6xGWKadwCRc8s.97.

Paul Brinkman, C. R. 2017. "Timeshare Companies Declare War on Cancellation Firms." Orlando Sentinel, August 14, 2017. http://www.orlandosentinel.com/business/brinkmann-on-business/os-bz-timeshare-cancellation-lawsuits-20170814-story.html.

Paul Brinkmann, C. R. 2017. "Timeshare-Law Change of Heart Lawsuit Involving Marriott Vacation Club." Orlando Sentinel, Junly 20, 2017. http://www.orlandosentinel.com/business/brinkmann-on-business/os-marriott-timeshare-legislation-20170719-story.html.

Redweek.com. 2016. "What Is the Best Way to Get Rid of My Timeshare?" Ask Redweek, September, 2016. https://www.redweek.com/resources/ask-redweek/get-rid-of-my-timeshare.

Sellmytimesharenow. 2016. "Timeshare in China Poised for Massive Growth." sellmytimesharenow.com, October 11, 2016. http://www.sellmytimesharenow.com/blog/timeshare-china-poised-massive-growth/.

Tacopino, J. 2017. "New York AG Reaches $6.5M Settlement with Manhattan Club." New York Post, August 17, 2017. https://nypost.com/2017/08/17/new-york-ag-reaches-6-5m-settlement-with-manhattan-club/.

Times, Y. 2018. "40 Million Tourists Visited Mexico in 2017." The Yukatan Times, March 11, 2018. http://www.theyucatantimes.com/2018/03/40-million-tourists-visited-mexico-in-2017/.

Weir, J., & Redweek. 2017. "Should Timeshare Owners Care About ARDA World? Developers Study Buyer Regret, Remorse, and Rescission." Redweek, April 2017. https://www.redweek.com/resources/ask-redweek/arda-world-timeshare-owners.

Weksler Law Group, P. 2017. "MANHATTAN CLUB OWNERS FINALLY GET VINDICATION - NY ATTORNEY GENERAL ANNOUNCES $6.5 MILLION SETTLEMENT WITH NY TIMESHARE DEVELOPER THAT SCAMMED PURCHASERS." Weksler Law Group, PPC, August 18, 2017. https://www.wekslerlawgroup.com/single-post/2017/10/13/MANHATTAN-CLUB-OWNERS-FINALLY-GET-VINDICATION---NY-ATTORNEY-GENERAL-ANNOUNCES-65-MILLION-SETTLEMENT-WITH-NY-TIMESHARE-DEVELOPER-THAT-SCAMMED-PURCHASERS.

ABOUT THE AUTHOR

 Wayne C. Robinson is an accomplished American author, captivating public speaker, and visionary film producer, whose mission is to inspire audiences worldwide to reach for their dreams. Growing up as an army dependent on military bases across the United States and Europe, Wayne's childhood was enriched with diverse experiences that shaped his perspective on life.

After graduating from the prestigious Munich American High School in Germany, Wayne pursued his higher education at both the renowned Berklee College of Music and the esteemed University of North Texas. His passion for storytelling led him to serve as a United States Navy journalist, where he honed his writing skills and developed a deep appreciation for the power of words.

In 1994, Wayne decided to embark on a path that combined his love for travel and connecting with people. Enrolling at the International Tour Management Institute (ITMI) in San Francisco, California, he set out to follow his dreams. This pivotal decision opened doors for Wayne to work with numerous esteemed resorts across the United States, Mexico, Caribbean islands, and Canada, serving as a seasoned sales and marketing representative. As his expertise grew, Wayne's dedication and talent were recognized, and he eventually earned the prestigious position of Director of Sales and Marketing for Prestige Travelers in Jamaica.

Wayne's exceptional achievements have garnered attention from major news media outlets in the United States, Canada, and the United Kingdom, thanks to his acclaimed book, "The African American Travel Guide." Additionally, Wayne is a prolific author, sharing valuable insights in works such as "How to Work in Vacation Hot Spots," "Change Your Thoughts Change Your Destiny," and "Job Hunting Secrets They Don't Tell You About." His literary contributions have reached readers around the globe, with his books available in over one hundred online bookstores.

Determined to utilize the power of storytelling to inspire change, Wayne C. Robinson ventured into the realm of film production. As the producer and director of the visionary project, "THE DREAMS LIVE ON," he strives to uplift hearts and minds through compelling visual narratives.

With a remarkable journey spanning across continents, Wayne C. Robinson continues to captivate audiences with his boundless enthusiasm, unwavering passion, and unwavering commitment to empowering others to pursue their dreams. Through his written words, engaging speeches, and inspiring film endeavors, Wayne leaves an indelible mark on the world, motivating countless individuals to dare to dream and make those dreams a reality.

INDEX

Made in United States
Troutdale, OR
02/29/2024

18081469R00146